SING THE HAPPY SONG!

SING THE HAPPY SONG!

(A history of Salvation Army vocal music)

by
Brindley Boon

Salvationist Publishing and Supplies, Ltd.,
117/121 Judd Street, London WC1H 9NN

The Salvation Army 1978
First published 1978
ISBN 0 85412 321 0

COLONEL BRINDLEY BOON
has been an officer since 1950 and after a period as a corps officer he
served in Editorial appointments at International Headquarters
(including a term as Editor-in-Chief), and in Canada. He has also
been National Secretary for Bands and Songster Brigades in the
British Territory. In 1976 he was appointed Executive Officer for the
International Congress 1978. The Colonel is a composer and
songwriter and more than 100 of his compositions have appeared in
print.

CONTENTS

CHAPTER ONE

A GLORIOUS HERITAGE
(1865-1878)

THE Salvationist was singing his stirring martial melodies long before
he ever put the mouthpiece of a brass instrument to his lips. The song
of the Christian Missioner was often a cadence of triumph as he with
his fearless comrades closed ranks and marched on in spite of brutal
attack, bitter scorn and ruthless ridicule.

In one town, where the pioneers had been forbidden to march
singing through the streets, a handful of supporters, not yet fully
persuaded to throw in their lot with the Mission, walked on the
pavement singing the songs of victory while the plainly uniformed
warriors marched in silence through the crowd-lined streets. This is the
Salvationist's vocal heritage—a glorious heritage.

What did they sing on Mile End Waste in those early days? What
songs did William Booth inherit from the members of The East
London Revival Mission who had persuaded him to become their
leader?

The fires of spiritual awakening that swept England in 1859 were
still burning brightly in 1865. People not usually given to religious
fervour were caught up in the flames and a new brand of Christianity
was presented. In their interests the form and ritual of the established
Church were abandoned and with them went the hymns.

The influence of the great American revivals had spread to Britain
and the new converts had taken up the happy, rhythmic compositions
imported from across the Atlantic. Such popular gospel songs as 'In
the sweet by and by', 'There is a fountain filled with Blood' and
'When the roll is called up yonder' immediately caught on and played
their important part in attracting new members to the ever-increasing
religious groups.

It is trite to say that The Christian Mission was born in the open air,
but it is an irrefutable fact. William Booth found his destiny at a
gospel meeting near 'The Blind Beggar' public house in Mile End
Road. It is true that meetings were also being held in a tent erected in
a Quaker burial ground in Whitechapel, but when the wind tore the
tent to pieces the only alternative meeting place that could be
procured was Professor Orson's Dancing Academy in New Road,
known more politely by its proper name, the Assembly Rooms.

1

Here three Sunday meetings were held, each preceded by an open-air meeting. The pages of William Booth's diary for 1865 throw fascinating light on the first recorded evidence of Christian Mission music-making. After giving information that the morning open-air 'preaching' was held at the Whitechapel end of New Road and in the Commercial Road in the afternoon, the 36-year-old evangelist reveals that in the evening an 'excellent service' was held in Mile End Road, when 'hundreds appeared to listen with undivided attention'. He goes on:

> We then formed a procession and sang down the Whitechapel Road to the Room. We had an efficient band of singers, and as we passed along the spacious and crowded thoroughfare, singing 'We're bound for the land of the pure and the holy' the people ran from every side. From the adjacent gin palaces the drinkers came forth to see and hear; some in mockery joined our ranks; some laughed and sneered; some were angry. The great majority looked on in wonder, while others turned and accompanied us as on we went, changing our song to 'There is a fountain filled with Blood' and then again to 'With a turning from sin let repentance begin!'
>
> The hall was filled. The power of the Holy Ghost was with the word. Three-fourths of the audience stayed to the after-meeting.

Could this have been the first time the singing missioners went 'on the march'? But 'The Eden Above', as the tune is called in Salvation Army music, is in 3/4 time and bands of today would not find it easy to march to this rhythm. How did the Christian Missioners of 1865 manage it?

In fairness we must admit that William Booth did not say they marched. They *passed along* the Whitechapel Road. In the ecstasy of their witness there would be no connection between the music and the movement. They possibly shuffled two steps here, hovered on one foot there, while others took three paces to catch them up.

Marches may have come with the Army and its bands, and with marches came 'marching time'. But in 1865 there would be no drum tap and no left foot for the accented beat; only a happy crowd singing its way from 'The Blind Beggar' to the dancing room, pilgrims on their way to the 'land of the pure and the holy'.

In this simple and unrehearsed way those singers that night set the pattern for all Salvation Army open-air activity and established the principle of the priorities of the Movement's vocalists. 'We're bound for the land . . .'—the testimony. 'Say will you go to the Eden above?'—the appeal. This is the blueprint, unalterable and everlasting.

There is no doubt that William Booth was fond of this song. It had the honoured first place in many earlier publications, including his 'Revival Songs' and The Salvation Army 'Penny Song Book'.

Lieut.-Colonel Richard Slater, the 'Father of Salvation Army music', said: 'This song is not of Army origin, but surely no people have sung it so often at outdoor and indoor meetings as have Army folks. Vast numbers, hearing the pointed questions from the lips of Salvationists, have been led to leave the way of sin and take the upward road to heaven'.

This song certainly set the Army marching, not only in the East End of London, but in many parts of the world.

It was used in the first Salvation Army meeting held in New York City led by Commissioner George Scott Railton and the seven Hallelujah lasses who had recently arrived from England to 'open fire' on the American continent.

The meeting was held in March 1880, in Harry Hill's Variety Theatre and was followed by the 'panorama of "Uncle Tom's Cabin"'. Railton led and one of the young women 'intoned a hymn in a high tremulous voice, dropping her "hs" and inserting "ahs" with a rising inflection as she raised herself on her toes in a manner that made the irreverent audience laugh'.

The report went on: 'The hymn as she read it invited the "'appy pilgrim" to go to the Eden above, and the concluding refrain, "We will go", sung by the whole army, was applauded with energy'.

When Hanna Ouchterlony and Jenny Svenson held the first meeting in a Stockholm theatre to the accompaniment of the latter's guitar, they sang 'We're bound for the land . . .'. That was in December 1882.

When Major Frederick Tucker, Captain Henry Bullard and their two assistants 'invaded' India in the same year they marched from the dockside singing and playing this same song. When 19-year-old George Pollard and 20-year-old Edward Wright conducted the first open-air meeting in New Zealand at the Fountain, Dunedin, on 1 April 1883, 'We're bound for the land . . .' was again chosen.

The song was also used when the Army 'opened fire' in Denmark (May 1887), Norway (January 1888) and Finland (November 1889). There is an interesting incident connected with the opening in Norway.

In the 1880s the message of this song reached the ears and heart of a young Norwegian woman working in England. It brought about a turning point in her experience. Soon after, she became a Salvationist and Corps Sergeant-Major at Portsmouth Corps. Later she returned to her home town of Stavanger.

On the very day that William Booth held a meeting in Oslo (25 October 1887)—a few months before the official opening of the Army in the country—she conducted an informal Army meeting in

Stavanger. It is almost certain that she used 'We're bound for the land . . .' on that occasion.

This woman, who later became Mrs Jeanna Corneliussen, was severely injured during riots in England and suffered greatly until her promotion to Glory in January 1940. She was one of the pioneer party which opened fire in Norway early in 1888. The leader of the party was a noted vocalist and song-writer from England, Staff-Captain Albert Orsborn, who arrived carrying his two-year-old son, one day to be the Army's sixth General, in his arms.

The song is indirectly linked with the opening of Army work in Australia. In July 1878, Edward Saunders, a Yorkshire stonemason and builder, was converted in Bradford after hearing James Dowdle, then in charge of the local Mission station, sing 'We're bound for the land . . .' at a street corner, accompanying himself on the violin. Saunders sailed for Australia the following year and with John Gore, another Christian Mission convert, from London, begged William Booth to send a Captain, preferably Dowdle, to commence the work 'down under'.

To these requests the Chief of the Staff (Bramwell Booth) replied that as Captain Dowdle had just been appointed to the Tyne Division he could not be released, but that the question of sending someone else was being 'prayerfully considered'.

Dr William Hunter, a Methodist Episcopal minister in Ohio, USA, could not have realized that his song, written in 1842, would have such a world-wide influence. His knowledge of its spiritual effectiveness was confined to hearing local farmers sing it as they drove along the roads to the gospel meetings, using it as a challenge to the more worldly-wise farmers working in the fields.

The author did not live long enough to realize its power in The Christian Mission and later The Salvation Army. He died in 1877.

That was the year when the Rev William Booth, General Superintendent of The Christian Mission, delivered his memorable address on 'Good Singing' at the Annual Conference. The verbatim report on the discourse occupied eleven pages of *The Christian Mission Magazine* for August 1877 and makes fascinating and informative reading even after 100 years.

Booth was a great champion of good singing, which, to please him, had to be congregational, hearty and useful. He had strong views on the subject. He rigidly condemned the practice of 'selecting a few people, converted and unconverted . . . to lead the congregation just because they happen accidentally to have melodious voices'.

Doubtless he had experienced some difficulty with organized choirs in the early days of his ministry. He had, he told the conference, 'ever found choirs to be possessed of three devils, awkward, ugly and impossible to cast out. They are the quarrelling devil, the dressing devil, and the courting devil, and the last is the worst of the three!'

He went on:

> Merely professional music is always a curse and should you ever find a choir in connection with any hall in this mission, I give you my authority to take a besom and sweep it out, promising that you do so as lovingly as possible.
>
> You must sing good tunes. Let it be a good tune to begin with. I don't care much whether you call it secular or sacred. I rather enjoy robbing the devil of his choice tunes, and, after his subjects themselves, music is about the best commodity he possesses. It is like taking the enemy's guns and turning them against him.
>
> However, come it whence it may, let us have a real tune, that is, a melody with some distinct air in it, that one can take hold of, which people can learn, nay which makes them learn it, which takes hold of them and goes on humming in the mind until they have mastered it. That is the sort of a tune to help you; it will preach to you, and bring you believers and converts.

The address concluded, the conference was open for discussion. Among those who took the floor were Christian Mission stalwarts Job Clare, William Garner and James Dowdle. Not all approved of their leader's sentiments and they said so. The first-named did not hesitate to regard himself as a singer. 'If you don't think I can sing, I do', he said and became critical of some of the Mission's leading of singing. Garner did not claim to be a soloist, but claimed to know something about leading congregations and organizing processions.

Dowdle, a gifted and soulful singer, heartily supported William Booth. 'Rant I am disgusted with', he declared, 'but Mission singing I love. I have never known it to fail to get a congregation in the open-air'.

He revealed that he had been to hear Sankey sing, and he sang 'The ninety and nine'. 'But I had expected more than I heard', he said. 'I did not think very much of his singing, but I saw where his power lay—he sang the words and the people caught them and got blest'.

The Founder's strong feelings on the subject led him for a considerable time to forbid any other but congregational or solo singing. The first *Orders and Regulations for Field Officers* decreed that: 'One voice alone is always much to be preferred . . . because the words can be heard with so much greater distinctiveness'.

Hardly had these regulations been circularized before the very thing William Booth condemned was, without warning, put into use, thus proving that the General's fears about the words not being heard when sung by a musical group were quite unfounded. It began with the Fry family.

CHAPTER TWO

A SINGING ARMY
(1878-1898)

IN May 1878, with a flourish of William Booth's pen, The Christian Mission became The Salvation Army. It had been an army in all but name for a long time.

Some five years before, in January 1873, George Scott Railton had written to 'My dear General' and signed himself 'Your ever-to-be Lieutenant'. In September of that year Railton was appointed the General Secretary of The Christian Mission.

In 1877 Elijah Cadman, in charge of Christian Mission work at Whitby, called for men and women to join the 'Hallelujah Army', signing himself 'Captain Cadman' at the bottom of the poster. When William Booth paid his first visit to the new opening, people were invited to come and hear 'The General of The Hallelujah Army'.

But the official documentary alteration took place in the Founder's bedroom in the Booths' Hackney home, whither Railton and young Bramwell Booth had been summoned for the customary morning business session. Railton presented a printer's proof of the Mission's 1878 report and appeal. On the front page, in bold type, it stated 'The Christian Mission . . . is A Volunteer Army'.

In *These Fifty Years* Bramwell Booth has recorded his reaction to the statement: 'Volunteer! I'm not a volunteer. I'm a regular or nothing'. Railton reports that William Booth also objected to the phrase. 'No', he said, 'we are not volunteers, for we feel we must do what we do, and we are always on duty'. He then, without further comment, crossed the room, put his pen through 'Volunteer' and above it wrote 'Salvation'.

'From the moment the Army received its title', wrote W. T. Stead years afterwards, 'its destiny was fixed. The whole organization was dominated by the name'.

One of the first innovations was the introduction of brass instruments into Salvation Army worship. The pioneering honours in this realm go to the Fry family of Salisbury. The story has been told fully elsewhere.

When Charles Fry gave up his business as a master builder and, with his sons, Fred, Ernest and Bert, left Salisbury at Whitsuntide,

6

1880, to join the Founder's staff at the Army's headquarters in Whitechapel, the family brought to their new task more than ability to play brass instruments. It was not long before, in the campaigns in which the Frys took part—many of them associated with the opening of corps—they were introduced as a male vocal quartet and in this way were used by God to win hundreds of souls for His Kingdom.

Henry Edmunds, who with Mrs Sarah Sayers had opened the work in Salisbury and was still there when the Frys began to attend meetings, described the father as a 'musician and missionary; singer and saint'. He remembered his service as a vocal soloist in the Founder's meetings and also the effectiveness of the quartet in its singing contributions in four-part harmony.

Ernest and Bert Fry were able shorthand scribes. The elder brother, Fred, was a Tonic sol-fa expert. When a new song was heard the words would be swiftly taken down while the melody was recorded. By this means an extensive repertoire was collected.

In his diary Fred Fry records: 'We arrived in Lancaster on the Saturday and, ascertaining the time and place of the meeting, went about twenty minutes early and started up the tune, "Just before the battle, mother", using the words of "Hark! the gospel news is sounding". By the time the soldiers assembled we had got the meeting "on the swing"'.

Charles Fry served only three years as a Salvationist. It is said that he overworked himself for Christ as a private business man and when he joined the Army his activity for the new Movement never ceased. He suffered indifferent health for this entire period, mainly because of a fall he had received some years previously, and after he had recovered sufficiently to sing a solo in an Exeter Hall meeting in March 1882, he had a relapse. Rest was ordered but this instrumental and vocal pioneer was promoted to Glory at the home of Army friends in Scotland on 24 August 1882.

The sons were transferred to other work. Fred became secretary to Herbert Booth, the Founder's third son, who will feature prominently in this history; Ernest was appointed to similar responsibilities with the Salisbury pioneer, Colonel Edmunds, by this time in charge of the work in Scotland; and Bert migrated to Australia.

The end of this brief chapter was but the beginning of group singing in the Army. Despite the Founder's misgivings and outspoken comments, the revolution had already begun, almost unnoticed.

With the opening of the National Barracks at Clapton as a training home in May 1882 came a considerable development in the annals of Salvation Army vocal history. When Herbert Booth, not yet twenty-one, was appointed to assist his brother Ballington, who was in charge of training men cadets, the idea of selecting a group of singers to tour Britain was formulated.

This resulted in the formation of a singing brigade, under the title of Salvation Songsters, which set out from Clapton in July 1883, the three-fold function being to win souls for Christ, to enlist the interest of young people in officership and to raise money for the training of cadets. Herbert Booth led this brigade of mixed voices throughout its six campaigns.

One of the members was Richard Slater, who had recently taken up an appointment in the newly-formed Music Department. It was his responsibility to find the voices and to teach the parts. Some of the Army's best songs were written during this association between Herbert Booth and Slater.

Another member was Fred Fry. Hearing that this young man could play a harp—an instrument he had learned to play at a billet whilst campaigning with other members of his family—Herbert Booth bought him one. He quickly became proficient and contributed in no small degree to the useful service of the singers.

The songsters were not on the road all the time. After a tour lasting some six weeks they would return to Clapton, some for a short period before being commissioned as officers and others being sent immediately on to the field, their training consisting of service with the singing brigade.

In the leadership of the campaigns Herbert was often assisted by his sisters, Emma and Eva, the former in charge of the women's side of the training garrison and the latter her assistant. The contribution to the Army's treasury of song of these gifted members of a remarkable family will be dealt with in a later chapter. These 'bands' of singing evangelists continued to tour until the winter of 1885.

The introduction of the 'Speaking, Singing and Praying Brigade' came in 1886. In March of that year an important rearrangement of the training system was made. Instead of cadets entering the homes in driblets at various times and being sent out to the field as officers in like manner, they entered at half-yearly intervals.

Three months were spent in undergoing training in the homes, and then a similar period was devoted to practical experience on the field, under the direction of training home officers. The first of the field sessions set the pace and for this the cadets were divided into brigades, all farewelling in grand style from Clapton on 24 February 1886.

The entire company was named the Household Troops and there was an air of excitement as the Founder dedicated them for this new imaginative venture. The cadets were formed into:

1. Three 'flying squadrons' of women cadets.
2. 'Cavalry corps forts' (caravans furnished to accommodate twelve persons each).
3. A party that travelled by Irish 'jaunting car'.
4. A speaking, singing and praying brigade under the leadership of Commandant Herbert Booth.
5. A 'flying column' of eighty men who marched, headed by their band, through Essex, Suffolk and Norfolk.

Each battalion, in turn, marched in front of the platform to be reviewed by the General, who took the salute. Distinctive insignia were worn. Officers in charge were called to the front to receive from the hand of the General a sealed envelope containing instructions about the means of travel and the route to be taken.

On the following Monday, 1 March, crowds gathered in Linscott Road to see the campaigners off on their voyages of holy adventure. The Speaking, Singing and Praying Brigade left at noon for King's Cross Station to take a train to Cambridge, the first stop on their journey up the west coast to Glasgow, and then north as far as Thurso, returning via Edinburgh and then to Tyneside, Wearside and further stops at Birmingham and other centres.

At Manchester the campaign meetings were held in the Free Trade Hall, and when Commandant Herbert Booth discovered that the grand organ could be used Fred Fry was instructed to play it. 'This was an instrument I had never played', records the 'voluntary' organist. 'I drew a plan of the composition pedals, discovered what each could be used for, launched out in faith and was able to give a good account of myself.'

The visit to Glasgow was particularly interesting. Here the Commandant and brigade were joined by Miss Emma and Miss Eva, who took leading parts in the proceedings. 'Professor' Slater, as the Commandant humorously introduced him, testified that his was a happy religion; he had something which made life worth living and gave him something to talk about in society other than the weather.

A feature was the contribution of 'Little Dot', of the training home nursery. She was the centre of attraction as she kept time to every song with her hands and sang her solo during the taking of the collection.

'Hers was a sweet baby voice', says Staff-Captain Blanche Cox, a member of the training homes staff who vividly reported the whole of the 60-day campaign for the benefit of *War Cry* readers, 'scarcely audible at first, but gaining confidence later on . . . Dot is only three years of age, and is already in training to be a good soldier of King Jesus, in Salvation Army service'.

The Glasgow campaign ended with a 'Great battle of song' in the

City Hall, at which the Fry brothers, Fred and Ernest, shared duties at the grand organ.

Herbert Booth, in a powerful address, declared that no one had a right to sing lively tunes except they were saved; that the devil had no claim to even as much as a demi-semi-quaver of music, and that he had been helped to usurp this power by Christians who put unsaved people up to sing the most sacred words.

The welcome home to all the Household Troops took place at Clapton Congress Hall on 3 May, barely three weeks before the beginning of the first International Congress.

Even with the undoubted success of the Speaking, Singing and Praying Brigade, William Booth was reluctant to approve of organized part-singing in corps activity. 'Choirs' were still frowned upon and it was taking a long time for William Booth to overcome his deep-rooted prejudice.

This did not prevent 'underground movements' springing up at many corps in Britain and overseas. Several well-known songster brigades of today can trace their beginnings to a date long before such sections were commissioned. This has led to considerable confusion and indecision in official quarters to recognize any one brigade as being formed before another.

History must, however, tell its own story, and credit be given to the real pioneers in organized part-singing in the Army's ranks.

The corps at Newton Abbot, in Devon, claims that its songster brigade was formed in 1882 under the leadership of Richard Bowden, who was recognized as Songster Leader when the section was commissioned some years later. It is apparent that this leader remained in charge for more than forty years and was succeeded by his deputy, Leslie Hasking, who led the brigade for more than twenty-five years.

Although the brigade at Springburn was formed officially in 1909, the corps is said to have had a singing brigade since 1894. Colonel Arthur Goldsmith, who as a young officer was stationed in Scotland, was one of the earliest vocal instructors there.

The history of organized singing in the corps at Scarborough dates back to 1887, and in 1891, at Luton Temple, a group of vocalists was enlisted as a party under the leadership of the Commanding Officer, Captain Clifton Bailey.

The following year saw singing brigades introduced at Nunhead, Tunstall and King's Cross. At the last-named corps the group was led by Brother Alex Dalziel, father of four gifted sons, Alex, William, Albert and Fred, each of whom became well known in Army music circles. Commissioner Geoffrey Dalziel is a grandson.

Before becoming a Salvationist, Brother Dalziel had been a

chorister at a Presbyterian Church in the district where he lived and was a member of the Royal Choral Society.

Commissioner William Dalziel remembered fifteen to twenty comrades coming to his home twice a week to learn songs from the early issues of *The Musical Salvationist*. As in so many other cases the group was disbanded when news of its activities reached official ears.

Beginnings at Nunhead were rather more subtle. At first a timbrel band was formed to provide interest for the single young women of the corps while the young men interested themselves in banding. A strict regulation was that the sisters were required to leave upon marrying, a rule that was later annulled.

It seemed natural that these enthusiasts should want to sing as they manipulated their timbrels, and when the help of some of the brothers was enlisted to provide support to the female voices, a singing brigade came into being. No great impression was made until 1905, when a promising song-writer, Oliver Cooke, became the leader. The section soon developed into one of the best-known in London.

Songster Leader Cooke remained in charge for some years before transferring to Lewisham, where a long period was served in charge of the songster brigade.

A brigade was formed at Tunstall in 1892 and did good service for some sixteen years. The leader and members could not see the need to wear uniform, but wise counselling eventually prevailed and at the time songster brigades were officially recognized the brigade was re-formed on constitutional lines, some of the earlier 'rebels' regretting the folly of their ways and becoming happy members of the new section.

In 1894 a singing brigade came into being at Brighton Congress Hall, the astute Commanding Officer presented blank commissions with appropriate wording to substantiate the inauguration. This did not make it right in the eyes of Headquarters, but Brighton has never retracted its claim to be the Army's first commissioned songster brigade!

The following year a brigade was formed at Belfast Citadel, but was re-established on more orthodox lines in 1897. In this way this old corps claims to possess the first songster brigade in Ireland, just as Springburn reckons to hold the honour in Scotland.

At Brixton, in South London, a singing brigade was founded by Colonel Herbert Jackson in 1896. A picture of this original section, published in *The Musician* in 1940, reveals the versatility of the personnel. The six women in the group are wearing a variety of continental costumes and a cello, violin, banjo and two mandolins add to the interest.

The costumes were obviously worn for a functional purpose connected with the brigade's activities. Could the success of this venture have persuaded Colonel Jackson to introduce this colourful attraction into the programmes of the International Staff Songsters, which he formed the following year?

CHAPTER THREE

SONGSTERS ARE COMMISSIONED
(1898-1978)

THE Army's first Commissioner, George Scott Railton, was a man of strong conviction and outspoken challenge. These qualities, so necessary in the formative years of the Movement, when his influence was third only to that of William and Catherine Booth, were later to get him into trouble, but none questioned his integrity nor lost respect for him.

He was a salvation warrior long before the change of name. In February 1874, within a year of joining, he published the Mission's first war song. It is probable that he wrote it.

The song, 'Christian rouse thee, war is raging!', set to the Welsh tune, 'Men of Harlech', appeared in its complete form in *The Christian Mission Magazine*. No indication of the author was given. It became known among Mission members as 'our war song', and the song breathed so much of Railton's adventurous spirit that it could indeed have been from his pen.

Later that year Railton wrote an article on the subject of singing. He firmly believed that, properly used, music would enhance the message of salvation that Booth preached, and he concluded his article with: 'Let us rescue this precious instrument from the clutches of the devil, and make it, as it may be made, a bright and lively power for good.'

The appeal was taken up at the 1874 conference of The Christian Mission. A motion was passed that 'many of our female converts could be most profitably formed into bands of singers to visit the homes of people as well as more publicly sing of salvation'.

Previous chapters have shown that William Booth was in no hurry to put the motion into practice. The 'bands of singers' were a long time in coming, and even the outstanding success of Herbert Booth's Speaking, Singing and Praying Brigade did not herald the recognition of commissioned songster brigades.

It must have been apparent by the early 1890s that organized vocal activity in the Army was rather inconsistent. Singing brigades were permitted to function in one place, but refused permission somewhere else. Certain songs were encouraged here, but discouraged there.

13

Perhaps it was concern for this variety of standards which prompted a *War Cry* reader to ask: 'Should not The Salvation Army have well-trained choirs as well as bands?'

The editor replied in the issue dated 26 November 1892: 'We certainly cannot see any objection in principle to a certain number of soldiers associating together, with the sanction of the Captain, for the purpose of taking a prominent part occasionally in salvation singing. Of course, the songs and music must be provided by The Salvation Army.'

A cautionary note was then introduced, perhaps at the instigation of a higher authority. The editor went on: 'But the whole drift of choirs, in our judgment, is to confine the singing to the few, instead of making it the servant of many, and until the danger is less we advise all corps to be guided by their leaders.'

However guarded it might have been, this statement was regarded at least as semi-official approval. Kilmarnock 1 Corps, in Scotland, had its own singing brigade by the end of that year and others followed the example.

Something had to be done. Some leading officers felt that such a useful weapon of evangelism should not be ignored, and it was Commissioner John Carleton who spoke to General Booth on the subject. As a result, he was given authority to form a songster brigade at his own corps, Penge, in South London, as an experiment.

On a Sunday in September 1898, twenty-four soldiers of the corps who had first met as a singing brigade that week, commenced conducting their own afternoon and evening open-air meetings with the Commissioner as their sergeant. In this way they fitted naturally into the corps brigade system in operation at many of the larger corps at that time.

On this occasion they sang an original song written by Adjutant Ruth Tracy to 'Annie of the vale', a Christy Minstrel melody, and an old song to a new tune, 'Isle of beauty'.

To help the indoor singing a large American organ was obtained. At the brigade's golden jubilee celebrations in 1948 Mrs Ada Taylor (née Bradbrook), who had been the first organist, recalled the Commissioner handing her a manuscript copy of 'Come, ye disconsolate' to be 'deciphered and learned'. The song was the first to be sung in public by the brigade.

Commissioner Carleton served as songster leader for two periods in the brigade's history, retiring for the second time in 1926, but to him must go the honour of being the Army's first commissioned songster leader. Other well-known personalities who have wielded the baton at Penge include Lieut.-Colonel Joseph Reardon, Colonel Harry

Coote, Samuel Hurren (son of the Commissioner bearing the same name), Terence Reardon (a son of the former leader) and Senior-Major Edward Saywell.

If the Penge Songster Brigade earned the right to become recognized as the Army's first official vocal section it was 'only just'. The same month which marked its formation also saw the beginning of a songster brigade at Clapton Congress Hall.

This was at the request of the Commanding Officer, Captain Charles Rich, who was later to become a Commissioner, Territorial Commander in Canada and Sweden and finally British Commissioner. The first leader was Major Edith Rogers and she was assisted by Staff-Captain Bessie Higgins, sister of General Edward Higgins.

The singers first met for practice in a small ante-room at the Clapton Temple. Securing suitable music created difficulties, but the Major, conferring with Commissioner Carleton and benefiting greatly from his Penge experiences, arranged many stirring pieces. These were painstakingly copied and duplicated on a gelatine mimeograph—'a sticky and unsatisfactory business', stated the Major.

Notwithstanding her difficulties in producing the music, Major Rogers found time to issue a weekly pamphlet dealing with songster matters which she proudly called 'The Clapton Warbler'.

Songster (later Colonel) Railton Howard began to help at practices by playing the violin. He became deputy songster leader and in 1902, when Major Rogers's precarious health made it necessary for her to relinquish the position, he was commissioned songster leader. This appointment he held for two years until the Major was able again to take up her duties.

Major Rogers continued to lead the brigade until her retirement in 1919, but continued to take a lively interest in vocal activity at the corps until her promotion to Glory.

Other leaders have included Adjutant Sifleet, George Downes and Alfred Ives. General Albert Orsborn was an early-day member.

The claims of Penge and Clapton Congress Hall have always been hotly contested by Lewisham, as well as Brighton Congress Hall and Kilmarnock. It is true that commissions were issued to the Lewisham Brigade long before the other sections were commenced, but these were not properly printed for the purpose and therefore were not officially recognized. This does not detract from the long and excellent service of this brigade, which has added its own chapter to the fascinating history of Army vocal music.

Although the corps at Manchester Citadel (formerly Manchester Openshaw) is said to have possessed a singing party soon after its opening in 1882, an official songster brigade was not formed until

1898 when Commissioner George Langdon, then an Ensign, was the Commanding Officer. This inauguration began a record of eighty years' outstanding service.

Under the leadership of Harry Salthouse, who was in charge for twenty-eight years until his retirement in 1970, the brigade progressed in musical efficiency and vocal technique until it became one of the best-known sections in the Army world. A campaign in Scandinavia in 1966 added to its reputation. The brigade is continuing to maintain a high standard under the direction of Songster Leader Frank Crowhurst.

The retired leader is by no means 'on the shelf'. Upon relinquishing his duties he became young people's band leader, and is now bandmaster. And this apart from responsibilities associated with his managership of the Manchester branch of Salvationist Publishing and Supplies Ltd.

Another brigade that made its first appearance in 1898 was the Borough. Although its beginnings and details of early leadership are obscure, there is no doubt that in the first years of its existence a useful function was fulfilled in this notorious Elephant and Castle district of London. For some time the corps has been amalgamated with Kennington Lane and known as Southwark Citadel.

These then were the pace-setters in that first year of Army songster service. Other groups quickly came into being, but there was no great rush. Gradually, and probably after a great deal of thought, songster brigades were formed and there is space in this history to highlight only those sections which, for one reason or another, have become household names. This is no disrespect to the others, whose service can surely be judged by its results.

One of the earliest brigades was that at Nottingham Memorial Halls (formerly Nottingham 1). Here Songster Leader William Hutchinson was in charge for many years and later Herbert Page continued the excellent work begun by his predecessors.

It was not until more than ten years after the introduction of songster brigades that one was formed in Bristol. This is surprising but easily explained by the fact that as early as 1896 a group of divisional songsters was inaugurated. This operated for a number of years under the direction of Divisional Songster Leader F. J. Yabsley.

The brigade was very much in the news and was regularly featured in the pages of *The Bandsman and Songster*, forerunner of *The Musician*. Programme construction was original and interesting and specialing was carried out at frequent intervals at corps in the widely spread division. Several attempts were made to organize similar groups in Britain, but none proved so successful or lasted as long.

The first corps brigade in Bristol was formed at Bristol Citadel and for many years efficient vocal sections have been in existence at Bristol Staple Hill and Bristol Easton as well as the parent corps. Staple Hill particularly has an excellent record of service. The Songster Leader for many years was George Phillips, who for a long period combined those duties with those of bandmaster, young people's sergeant-major and torchbearer secretary. He himself provided the brigade's accompaniment at the organ.

In July 1948 Harlesden Songster Brigade made history by becoming the first British brigade to campaign on the continent of Europe. Under the leadership of Major (later Colonel) Fred Grant it carried out an eight-day tour of the Netherlands and broadcast from Hilversum.

This brigade had a humble beginning in a Christmas caroling party in 1910 and four years later became the first songster brigade to provide a programme in a prison—at Wormwood Scrubs. The leader of that caroling party, Alfred Boon (father of the author of this history), has been given credit for founding the section, and subsequent leaders have included John Lyons, Albert Coe, Oliver Dimond and Will Sinnock.

Songster Leader Sinnock was in charge for thirteen years and after being invalided out of the forces lost his life whilst on fire guard in 1944, when his place of business in London was destroyed in an air raid. The brigade owes much to his enthusiasm and efficient training.

In 1953 Leigh-on-Sea Songster Brigade, under the leadership of Mrs Freda Lambert, visited Scandinavia and four years later Hanwell Songster Brigade campaigned in Switzerland. Songster Leader Sam Hooper led this West London brigade for more than twenty-five years and upon retirement from that position returned to his native Devon and became Songster Leader at Exeter Temple.

Sweden has been a 'happy hunting ground' for British brigades in recent years, visits having been made by Sutton (1958), Hillingdon (1969) and Morriston (1977).

The last-named campaign meant that the Morriston section passed into history as the first Welsh songster brigade to tour overseas. This leads naturally to the question, 'Which was the first songster brigade in Wales?'

This is not easy to answer. At a time when group singing was developing among Salvationists in England, their counterparts in the 'land of song' still held firm convictions about the effectiveness of casual, unrehearsed congregational singing. This was their heritage and such activity had played its powerful part in the Welsh revivals of the mid-nineteenth century and the launching of Salvation Army work in 1874.

It is likely, therefore, that an organized songster brigade did not appear in Wales until 1908, when such a section was formed at Merthyr Tydfil. In that year Captain Rogers, an officer serving with The Salvation Army Assurance Society, was transferred to the town and with his wife, a daughter and two sons became the nucleus of the new section.

Reference has been made to Belfast Citadel's claim to have been the pioneer songster brigade in Ireland. This section is able to chalk up another 'first' to its credit. In 1956 it travelled by plane to Scotland, thus becoming the first British songster brigade to fly to an appointment.

Springburn and Kilmarnock will have to share the honour of being the first in Scotland. Both had unofficial brigades before the year of recognition and it is assumed that both became official sections in 1898.

No reference to songster brigade history could be complete without reference to well-established sections which because of certain personalities associated with their leadership have made an indelible impression upon generations of Salvationist music-lovers. In this category one must include Harrow and Colonel Railton Howard; Regent Hall and Bandmaster Herbert Twitchin, who held the dual leadership role for many years; Chalk Farm and Songster Leader Edward Souter; and Upper Norwood and Colonel Bernard Adams.

The fact that these are all London brigades is not to suggest that there are no personalities anywhere else in Britain. The leaders mentioned were and are continually in the public eye and it cannot be denied that the 'big city' is still the focus of Salvationist attention.

To augment this formidable list one could well add Portsmouth Citadel, Castleford, Ashton-under-Lyne, Ilford, Aberdeen Citadel, Govan, Sheffield Citadel, Birmingham, Cardiff Canton, Sunderland Monkwearmouth—and a host of others.

The 1930s can rightly be regarded as the years when songster brigades grew in numbers and progressed in musical prowess. The pioneer festivals inaugurated in this decade will have space in a later chapter.

Since the end of the 2nd World War, however, there has been a leap forward in vocal efficiency. Able, dedicated young leaders are happily sharing the fruit of their acquired knowledge with eager vocalists, with what success all are aware. The names of Douglas Collin, Keith Prynn, Alfred Crowhurst and Muriel Yendell come readily to mind. There are many more.

CHAPTER FOUR

SONGS IN EUROPE

IT was Dr John Fulton, the eminent New York clergyman, who declared, 'These people will sing their way round the world'. William Booth referred to the words in 1886 when he said, 'The prophecy . . . is already being fulfilled, for on sea and on land the songs have been heard all round the globe already'.

If this was the case then how much more is it true today! Dr Fulton's prophecy has indeed been fulfilled and the happy songs of salvation are being sung in eighty-two countries, in more than 100 languages.

History has proved that whenever people have entered into a new spiritual experience they have wanted to sing about it and express their new-found happiness by this means of communication. Salvationists are no exception.

As soon as the Army flag was unfurled in a country the vocal history of that new opening began. In some places it took longer for organized sections to be recognized, but there was always the desire to sing.

France

With no open-air meetings or processions permitted when Catherine Booth (eldest daughter of the Founder and Army Mother and later known as the Marechale), assisted by Florence Soper (later Mrs Bramwell Booth) and Adelaide Cox, opened the work in France, another point of contact with the people had to be found. An answer was provided in the production and sale on the streets, under police licence, of *En Avant* ('Forward!'), the French equivalent of *The War Cry*.

Later, young women Salvationists visited cabarets, distributing literature, singing salvation songs and inviting the patrons to Army meetings.

Shortly after the courageous opening, nineteen-year-old Herbert Booth, the third son of the family, arrived in Paris to help his sister. This was a veritable baptism of fire for the youth and provided him with the unexpected opportunity of introducing Army music into France and of laying the foundations of his own considerable contribution to the Movement's song-making.

Many duties fell to Herbert's lot. He looked after the heating and lighting of the little hall; guarded the door; quelled the disturbances of the roughs; and whitewashed walls, scrubbed floors and cleaned paintwork. Years afterwards he boasted that he received his first black eye whilst serving as a doorkeeper in Paris!

A woman sympathizer suggested that for singing in the meetings some tunes of secular songs in her possession should be used. She felt that this would be good because the people would know the melodies.

But where were suitable words to come from? There were decided limitations in Herbert Booth's knowledge of the French language, but he ventured to make an attempt at supplying the needed verses. Unforeseen difficulties arose in the matter of metre and rhyme. Not to be deterred, the young man obtained a French hymn book, studied it carefully and so discovered the pattern for his first efforts as a songwriter.

It was, however, not until 1927 that *The Bandsman and Songster* announced the formation of France's first songster brigade. This was at Paris Central Hall and the commissioning ceremony was conducted by the Chief Secretary, Colonel Frank Barrett, who later returned to the territory as Territorial Commander and was interned during the 2nd World War.

The Songster Leader was Captain Francis Evans, now a Commissioner living in retirement in Switzerland. The ceremony evidently made an impression upon the reporter, for he was able to record such details as: 'A fine influence prevailed as the Chief Secretary, after handing over the commission and presenting an appropriate text to each songster, had them all to kneel while the divisional commander prayed for the blessing of God upon them'.

The corps officers were Captain and Mrs Henri Becquet, of Congo fame. The Captain said: 'We have great hopes that the brigade will set the pace and inspire other musical combinations in the territory.'

But the enthusiasm was shortlived. The idea did not catch on to the extent hoped, and organized singing in France has, in the main, been confined to vocal groups being formed on a temporary basis for special occasions.

Belgium

Little is known of Army musical beginnings in Belgium. There can be no doubt that Salvationists of this command have kept alive the interest in singing, both as a functional experience and as a cultural development.

An efficient songster brigade has been in existence at Brussels Central Corps for many years. For some time the leader was Captain

Francy Cachelin, then Editor of the Belgian *War Cry* and now, a Colonel, Chief Secretary for the British Territory.

The Captain, during his period in charge, encouraged the constant use of *The Musical Salvationist*, tackling the more difficult settings in the manner of British brigades. A highlight in this section's long history was the occasion when they sang to King Baudouin of the Belgians in 1960.

An efficient small guitar group also functions at this corps.

Switzerland

The pioneers in Switzerland were too busy fearlessly facing the fierce opposition and contesting legal injustices to record musical beginnings for the benefit of future historians. Every possible barrier was erected to prevent the Salvationists from holding any kind of meeting as well as gaining a foothold.

At the height of the legal battles a song was used to quash an earlier ruling—without a note being sung! Summonses issued by the police in Geneva were dismissed by the magistrate when the Army's lawyer read Psalm 150 in court as defence. The injunction to 'Praise ye the Lord' was never used to better effect.

This followed hard on an incident in Zürich when the Salvationists protested against the decree that a one-time dance hall must not be used for private meetings because the staircase had been used previously by dancers. The district court declared the decree 'unconstitutional'. The faithful warriors celebrated by immediately taking over the premises and lifting their voices and their hearts in a 'song of grateful praise'.

As with all continental countries the guitar has been a popular instrument in Switzerland. String brigades have been functioning since the earliest days of the Army and in many centres meetings cannot be visualized without them.

At the same time there has been a genuine attempt to popularize part-singing along the lines of British songster brigades. In 1914 such a section was inaugurated at Berne 1 under the leadership of Captain Emil Nigg, who later became the second Territorial Music Secretary. There were thirty members. Corps in Basle, Zürich and Geneva soon followed the example.

The first territorial songster congress was held in the Casino Hall, Berne, in 1956, amidst scenes of great enthusiasm. The events consisted of two festivals and three sessions of councils, more than 800 delegates, including string band members, attending.

The Chief Secretary, Colonel Charles Péan, led the gatherings, assisted by the Territorial Music Secretary, Senior-Major Herbert Silfverberg, who conducted the united singing.

Songsters selected from Berne 1 and Berne 2 amalgamated to carry out a tour in Britain in 1974 and to take part in the farewell meeting of General and Mrs Erik Wickberg in London's Royal Festival Hall. The General became an officer from Berne 2.

A vocal group from French-Switzerland was invited to represent the territory at the International Congress 1978 to be known as the Mountain Minstrels.

Germany

The Germans are a nation of singers. To hear a congregation in that land in full harmony is an inspiration. It is little wonder, then, that songster brigades progressed with greater speed than did brass bands, although it was well into the twentieth century before such sections were commissioned.

One of the first was at the Berlin Schonberg Corps. This was formed in April 1911 under the leadership of Ensign Sidney Treite. With his brother Percy, who became Bandmaster of the German Staff Band, the Ensign was involved in much of Army music-making in Germany and Switzerland.

Other members of that early brigade included Adjutant Sam Richards and Lieutenant S. Carvosso Gauntlett. The last-named, as a Lieut.-Commissioner and Germany's Territorial Commander, was promoted to Glory in 1961. His son, Caughey, is the present Territorial Commander.

The beginnings of Berlin Temple Songster Brigade could date from even earlier, but there is no confirmation of this fact. It is known that a virile section was flourishing soon after the armistice in 1918 and that under the territorial leadership of Colonel Mary Booth the brigade, with Adjutant Otto Doring as songster leader, was featured in many gatherings.

Particularly did the brigade earn a reputation for conducting Easter campaigns, during which the life of Christ, including His death and resurrection, was presented in song.

In 1926 an English editorial visitor reported his impressions of German singing. He especially singled out the fine congregational singing in a mammoth open-air meeting when, as Colonel Booth led 'Take Thou my hand and guide me', scores of bystanders made their way forward to kneel at the three drums the Colonel had caused to be placed in position as a Mercy Seat.

The reporter also wrote enthusiastically of the 'small but good' brigade at Hamburg 1 and that at Nuremberg, in Bavaria, a town much later to become associated with the aftermath of the 2nd World War.

After the cessation of hostilities in 1945 the Army in Germany made a miraculous come-back, as it had done in 1918. In the divided city of Berlin the uniform was soon recognized on the streets and few objections were raised.

For the visit of General and Mrs George Carpenter to Berlin in 1946, their last to the Fatherland, Colonel Doring formed a singing brigade which made helpful contributions to the meetings. Several similar groups of singers have come into being in the intervening years, and when General and Mrs Clarence Wiseman visited Germany in the winter of 1976, united songsters, with guitar accompaniment, took part in congress meetings held in Hanover.

Although the centre of Salvation Army activity has now shifted from Berlin to Cologne, crowds of Salvationists make their way from all parts of the country to the former capital for annual Repentance Day meetings. This tradition, started by William Booth himself, has been retained despite difficulties, and the singing is as effective as ever.

Guitar brigades continue to function, the first after the 2nd World War being formed at Berlin Schonberg in 1947.

On her last visit to Germany, Catherine Booth, the Army Mother, suggested, after hearing the united songsters in action, that English brigades would need to look to their laurels. One wonders what standard would have been reached had two cruel wars not intervened.

Italy

Toward the end of 1886 Staff-Captain James Vint was asked to go to Rome to report on the prospects of commencing Army work in Italy. This was in response to an urgent request from an English couple, Mr and Mrs Gordon, who had lived in the capital city for a long time and had their own mission hall. They were eager to hand over themselves and all they had to the service of the Army.

The Staff-Captain was a most versatile officer who could sing, play the violin and piano, compose music and write shorthand, in addition to speaking several languages, including Italian. For two years he had been working in his spare time among the organ-grinders of the Italian Colony in London at Clerkenwell, where he had established a corps.

He arrived in Rome in January 1887, armed with leaflets of songs which he had translated into Italian. Some of these were introduced at a family meeting held in the Gordon home on his first day in the city. As one of the songs was being sung two young men knelt at a sofa, which was thereby transformed into a Mercy Seat, to give their hearts to God. They became the first Salvationists in Italy.

This initial spiritual success seemed to set the divine seal upon the preliminary inquiries. Six weeks later, in London's Regent Hall, the newly promoted Major and Mrs Vint were dedicated by the General to open officially the work in Italy. At the first meeting, on 20 February, the Major's musical gifts were much in evidence as he accompanied the singing on a borrowed out-of-tune piano or, in more delicate moments, on his violin. Twenty-five people attended and sixteen of them 'stood up for pardon'.

Three years later Major Vint was assassinated when leaving a hotel in Brussels. It was thought that a member of a secret society who had knelt at the Mercy Seat in Rome had divulged some of its secrets to him and, in consequence, another member of the society had been deputed to murder Vint when the opportunity presented itself.

The Army's 'ambassador extraordinary', Commissioner Railton, once described something of the beauty of Italian singing when harnessed to the experience of the Salvationist. He wrote it in the May 1912 issue of *All the World* and said:

> In a little room in Genoa I experienced the sort of singing that I never yet heard in any cathedral: the triumph of a handful of those who had set out for conquests such as their townsman, Columbus, never imagined, singing, when they seemed to have nothing—
>
> > *Thou art enough for me,*
> > *Thou precious living, loving Lord,*
> > *Yes, Thou art enough for me.*
>
> But every precious memory of Italy was almost eclipsed by what I saw and heard among our mountaineers of Ariano and Faeto. I arrived in Naples after one of the most least agreeable voyages I ever made, from Alexandria.
>
> In the great city we had no hall, and I carried from it only a memory of squalor and sin, though some kind friends did their best to cheer me on my way. Beautiful and blessed little meetings in Ariano hardly prepared me for the surprise that was coming.
>
> At a little station on an almost unfrequented line to Italian tourists we found some comrades with mules awaiting us. Ignorant as I am to this day of the management of any sort of steed, it was quite a relief to find that the uphill climb before us forbade anything beyond a walk and that our animals well understood their way. The aspect of the whole surrounding country was so barren and stony that it was a continual wonder that people could make a living at all under such conditions.
>
> Yet we sang all the way up that two or three hours' climb, and when we were near to Faeto quite a large group of comrades was seen coming out to meet and greet us. They sang us a welcome home, and though nearly everybody in Faeto had that same aspect of rugged poverty that struck one so in the scenery, joy and song abounded all the time . . .
>
> The silent awe of the mass, varied by the singing of professionals hired from the opera, can never compete with the Franciscan chantings, or the guitar-

accompanied solos of our songsters to reach and capture and enrapture Italian souls.

The Netherlands

It was Commissioner Railton's search for someone to assist him in translating an English song book into Dutch for use by Salvationists in South Africa that took him to Amsterdam in February 1886. There he met Gerrit Govaars, who the previous year had appeared on the streets of Amsterdam wearing a pair of brass S's on the lapels of his coat.

Govaars, a government schoolteacher, had learned about The Salvation Army from a young friend in Paris and, impressed by all he had heard, decided to become 'one of them'—before he had even heard of the Articles of War or been sworn-in as a soldier under the Army flag.

It was surely more than coincidence that Railton was introduced to the Govaars family and was invited by Gerrit's widowed mother to stay with them. As Railton could not speak Dutch and Govaars could not speak English they had to converse in French, and it was by this means of communication that the young Dutchman learned all about the Army and Railton was able to answer his many questions.

After ten days, and when his many searchings for a translating assistant for the song book had failed, Railton returned despondently to London, taking with him the unemployed teacher. The plan was for Govaars to spend two or three weeks in England assisting with the work of translating, but this period was extended to three months.

During this time the 'Hallelujah Dutchman', as he came to be called, accompanied General Booth on several campaigns and participated in the first International Congress. He was permitted to wear uniform and was made a Lieutenant by the General himself.

Govaars was an able musician and when, in March 1887, he returned to the Netherlands to assist Captain and Mrs Joseph Tyler with the opening of the work, his violin came in useful to accompany the singing in the first meeting. He also wrote songs in several languages and composed music.

This territory has always favoured four-part singing, and songster brigades, in the English style, have existed since the early days. A great champion of progressive music in the Netherlands was Lieut.-Colonel J. P. Rawie. He was Bandmaster of the first National Band, formed in 1910, and continued his interest into retirement.

Another name for so long connected with Army music-making in the territory is that of Brigadier Gerrit Claeijs. He was placed in charge of the newly formed music section at Territorial Headquarters in 1930 and, with his wife, set about providing suitable songs for songsters, either writing and composing them (Mrs Claeijs provided the words) or translating from *The Musical Salvationist* issued in English from International Headquarters.

With the renaissance of Army music at the end of the 2nd World War, Major Douglas Rolls was appointed Territorial Music Secretary and, apart from his duties with the National Band, of which he was the Bandmaster, he sought to encourage the vocalists of the territory. Mrs Rolls, well known and respected as a vocalist and a former member of the Assurance Songsters, gave considerable help in this direction, her quick grasp and mastery of the language greatly aiding her endeavours.

During the service of Major Rolls the territory's first songster congress was held in Amsterdam. Brigades from Arnhem and Amsterdam 5 were featured in the Saturday festival, in which Mrs Major Rolls sang, accompanied by the National Band, 'O for a heart', the music composed by Brigadier William Palstra, the Training Principal, who later served as Territorial Commander and then as International Secretary for Europe at International Headquarters.

Salvationists of the Netherlands have ever striven to keep up to date with developing vocal trends. At the time of the drastic change of music introduced during the early 1960s a Salvation Army record hit the music world headlines in The Netherlands by achieving an LP sales record in that country of 112,000 copies. This beat most decisively such previous top hits as the Dutch version of 'My fair lady' (60,000 copies) and the sound track of 'West side story' (70,000 copies).

As a result of this success the Army gained the country's 'Golden Disc' award. The Territorial Commander, Commissioner Palstra, accepted the recognition on behalf of Salvationists in the Netherlands and, in response to the prolonged applause, said: 'Our meeting point is music. It has a special place in The Salvation Army and is one of our foremost methods of preaching the gospel of Jesus Christ'.

The record was named 'Jubileum Jubel' and the singers were the all-officer Jubilee Chorus, conducted by the Commissioner's son, William, at that time Holland's Territorial Music Secretary.

Central Europe

The handful of faithful singers who supported difficult pioneering work in Czechoslovakia, Hungary, Latvia, Estonia, Yugoslavia and Russia cannot be overlooked. Although Army activity has been suppressed in these lands, there is ample evidence that the spirit of those Salvationists lives on. Their singing cannot have been in vain.

Transferred from Germany to open the work in Hungary in 1924, Lieut.-Colonel Franz Rothstein had quickly to devise a scheme to bring him into contact with the people. Accompanied by two women-officers who had also been transferred from Germany, and armed with a guitar and ample supplies of *Segelykialtas (The War Cry)* he made a nightly visit to the cafes in Budapest.

As he moved between the tables people, falling under the spell of his charming personality, would smile, cease drinking and engage in conversation. Some of the orchestras would stop playing when he arrived and then the resourceful Colonel would enlist the help of his companions and strike up a happy song of Christian experience as copies of the paper were disposed of.

Austria

A London songster serving in turn at New Barnet, High Barnet and Kilburn Corps claims to have been the first Salvationist to be sworn-in as a soldier in her native Austria. She was converted in an Army meeting in Switzerland in the early 1920s and, returning to Vienna, was anxious to become a Salvationist. That was in 1925.

Attempts had been made on several occasions to secure a footing for Army work in that country, but without success. The strong Catholic element had made pioneering difficult.

This comrade wrote to Mrs Commissioner Elwin Oliphant, wife of the then Territorial Commander for Switzerland, whose writings had greatly helped in the development of her Christian experience, to seek advice as to what she should do. She was encouraged to make contact with Captain Selma Freud, then serving in Switzerland, who had been selected to assist Captain Lydia Saak in opening fire in Austria. Captain Freud was the sister of Sigmund Freud, the noted psychologist.

The convert, Kamilla Lovy, made the contact, returned to Vienna to await the pioneers and in 1927 became the first soldier.

A year before, she had been in the enthusiastic crowd which, at the city's West Station, greeted Lieut.-Colonel Mary Booth, Territorial Commander for Germany, and the German Staff Band as they arrived to provide a musical and spiritual prelude to the work. She followed as the march processioned along Mariahilferstrasse to the Methodist Church where the first meeting was held.

The song remembered on this occasion was not a bright, lilting Army ditty, but the more sedate and perhaps more suitable hymn of the Church, 'Take Thou my hand and guide me'. Colonel Rothstein, the singing pioneer in Hungary, was also present.

The Army has been in Austria for fifty years, its service unbroken since the opening reported above. The work there was first under the command of Czechoslovakia, then Germany, now Switzerland, and comrades from these countries have, over the years, crossed the border to give vocal support to the courageous Austrian minority, both in Linz and Vienna.

This was certainly the case in 1973 during the visit of General Erik Wickberg, the first international leader to visit Austria. The officers' band from Berne travelled 700 miles by road to take part in the meetings with its music and song.

1914 International Congress in London and to tour in Britain. Simply
to say that the singers did well is the understatement of the century.
Narraway's Minstrels, as they were informally called, swept all before
them and introduced a brand of presentation that became a talking
point around the Army world for years to come.

The singing was infectious and before long all the delegates were
walking in the streets of London unconsciously singing 'Goodbye
Pharaoh', 'Roll along Jordan' and other plantation songs. Salvationists
of the British Isles took the minstrels to their hearts and a tremendous
reception greeted them everywhere they went.

Two further tours in Europe were carried out by the brigade—in
1921 and 1925-6. On the first occasion a series of tours was arranged
and the party remained in Britain for nine months.

Methods adopted to make the best of the visit were most varied
and highly successful. Through crowded streets the West Indians
marched and at other times covered great distances on decorated
lorries. Floating banners and attractive announcements called attention to the party's presence and the object and extent of the
mission. Funds were raised for the advance of work in the West Indies.

The leader was Major Cecil Walker, who later became the first
West Indies officer to reach the rank of Lieut.-Colonel.

Captain and Mrs Ezekiel Purser joined the party for three months.
They, with their six-year-old daughter, were on the way to pioneer
work in Nigeria. The daughter, now Lieut.-Colonel Dorothy Purser,
Chief Secretary for the Caribbean Territory, remembers her childhood
excitement at the experience. She says: 'I recall vividly the reception
the singers had in response to the lilting West Indian songs, choruses
and Negro spirituals, which were unique in Army circles in those
days'.

The third tour also lasted nine months and coincided with an
international social conference and General Bramwell Booth's
seventieth birthday celebrations. The leader was Staff-Captain George
Morris and the proceeds went toward purchasing the training college
property which is still situated in Orange Street, Kingston.

'Pilgrim', writing in a Sheffield paper, reported:

> The singers are few in number but effective in song . . .
> 'I aint goin' to grieve my Lord no more!' was a lovely typical song. We cannot
> imagine anything more sweetly natural, more innocently impressive; the words
> fitted the singers and the singers suited the words.
> It was impossible to listen to them without being deeply affected by the simple
> melodies. Many of us left the citadel humming the haunting refrains. The book of
> words cost only two pennies and seeing it was adorned with portraits of the singing
> party, it was cheap at the price.

We also found ourselves humming over the words during the quiet moments we spent later in our home. There is a fascination about the words which cannot be ignored.

There may never be another singing brigade quite like those happy minstrels, but the West Indies has its own proud record of God-blessed ministry. Perhaps inspired by the pioneers already referred to, divisional songster brigades were formed in the 1920's, it being easier to group a number of vocalists in this way than to encourage the introduction of smaller sections in isolated areas.

Typical of divisional songster brigades was the one at Guyana. Drawn from the four corps in Georgetown, Demerara, the songsters were used in campaigning in turn at the twelve corps in the division. The leader was Captain Dadd, a Jamaican, and the brigade's star piece was 'I've touched my finger on the golden pen'.

At the territorial centre corps songster brigades have been in existence for many years. A milestone in this history was the first music councils held in Kingston in 1956. The gatherings were led by the Territorial Commander (Lieut.-Commissioner Frank Ham) and the musical guests were Brigadier and Mrs Frank Longino, of the USA Southern Territory.

Well-planned councils catered for the practical needs of the delegates, and in the festival given in the Bramwell Booth Memorial Hall items were presented by three songster brigades from the city corps and the Chorus of the Institute for the Blind, and soloists.

The giant open-air gathering preceding the final meeting, followed by a march, stirred hundreds of people who thronged the streets of downtown Kingston. It was a thrilling sight as masses of white-clad Salvationists marched to the strains of hymn tunes and were followed by hundreds of people.

Eight miles off the coast of Guyana lies Devil's Island. The work of Commissioner Charles Péan in bringing hope, salvation and liberation to criminals imprisoned there is told elsewhere. The influence of holy song in this story of deliverance must have a place in this volume.

Just fifty years ago Ensign Péan was instructed to make his own report on conditions on the island and to inquire into the possibility of establishing Army work there. Returning to France he presented his frank findings, together with recommendations as to how The Salvation Army could help colonists.

It was not until 1933 that permission for the work to begin was granted. The then Major Péan, with three other officers from France, arrived with plans to break through to the men and not only serve them socially and morally, but spiritually as well.

Reported Charles Péan in *Devil's Island*: 'Every Tuesday evening the Captain gathers them for a private meeting. Some six or seven seat themselves around a table with their Bibles open before them. They read like children a few paragraphs, which the officer explains and comments upon. Songs are sung!'

Singing on Devil's Island! Major Péan could hardly have believed his ears. Here was a handful of converts actually singing. Recalling the life of devilry and debauchery these men had lived before the coming of the Army, he must have marvelled at the miracle of music in such a place.

The Army's work on Devil's Island is now a part of its history. The last of the criminals were repatriated in 1953, but it is fervently hoped that the song of deliverance, of courage, of strength born in those days in the hearts of sin-tarnished men who, before the coming of the Salvationists, considered their plight to be hopeless, is still ringing out.

Only eternity will reveal the influence of such music used in so dedicated a manner.

CHAPTER EIGHT

CANADIAN INTERLUDE

FOLLOWING the 'invasion' of New York by George Scott Railton and his 'magnificent seven', two of the lasses were left behind to carry on the work while the remainder of the party moved on to Philadelphia. There Railton caught up with the Shirley family and conferred the rank of Captain on each of them. Soon the leader was able to report to London that, after its first ten weeks in the USA, The Salvation Army had ten corps in operation and some 200 meetings weekly were being held.

The restless pioneer then proceeded to St Louis, Mo, to launch a western campaign. It was not easy to secure a hall, and when one was obtained for a meeting some of the congregation disgraced themselves by spitting on the floor. News of this reached owners of other halls who refused to let their premises for such a purpose.

At long last a sympathetic landlord was found and on Sunday, 2 January 1881, the first meeting was held. Three months later Railton was recalled to London, a summons that did not please him. He set his views fully before the General and when the reply, in the form of a cable, said simply, 'Come along!', he practised what he had always preached, saluted, gathered together his few possessions and left for England.

While on his way to Halifax, Nova Scotia, where he was to embark, Railton wrote a stirring song of consecration that has become an Army classic:

> No home on earth have I,
>   No nation owns my soul;
> My dwelling-place is the Most High,
>   I'm under His control;
> O'er all the earth alike
>   My Father's grand domain,
> Each land and sea with Him alike;
>   O'er all He yet shall reign.

The tune he used was 'A life on the ocean wave'.

Years later Richard Slater, the 'father of Salvation Army music', commenting on this song, said: 'Here we have in a few short lines what may be called the scheme of life, the philosophy of personal religion as understood and consistently applied by Commissioner

Railton. It is the voice of personal triumph of a spirit that has risen to higher levels than are marked by time and space; it defines an altitude of religious experience where, by a voluntary act, the soul becomes absorbed in its God'.

While walking through the streets of Halifax Railton felt impelled to witness to the people—and missed the boat! The next sailing was in ten days and the enforced delay was put to good purpose in the carrying out of a vigorous one-man campaign.

At one meeting a man named Charles Archard was converted and as the Army had not yet been established he joined the Methodist Church. It is probable that this man was the first Army convert in Canada. He became a respected business man and remained true to God for the rest of his life, serving for some years as an elder of his church.

During those ten days Railton tried out his new song on his congregation. They sang with gusto, but many of them seemed to prefer the original secular words! The singing of such intimate sentiments had the effect of confirming Railton in his own faith, and his loyalty to his leaders.

In that same year (1881) Jack Addie, an eighteen-year-old draper's assistant, settled with his parents in London, Ontario, from Jarrow-on-Tyne, England. The youth had met the Army in his North of England home town and the story of his first encounter has been written by Mrs General Carpenter:

> One night Addie was walking up the street with two or three chums when he saw a crowd of people at the top of a hill, jostling and shouting. He looked closer, and saw that a group of rough, hard-faced men were rolling a bundle down the hill. Propelled by the hands and feet of the men the bundle soon reached the bottom and then, much to Addie's consternation, this mysterious arrangement gathered itself together, stood up on its feet, shook itself all over and shouted in a stentorian voice 'Hallelujah!' while a jolly looking round face, set with a pair of laughing eyes, beamed up at 'these rude fellows of the baser sort' with unutterable love and sympathy.
>
> The bundle was none other than Captain John Lawley, and this was Jack Addie's introduction to The Salvation Army.

He was converted soon afterwards during a tempestuous meeting at Newcastle upon Tyne conducted by Captain Gipsy Smith.

With such a background it was not surprising that young Addie should miss the Army when he arrived in London, Ontario. He missed the stirring meetings, the thrilling testimonies, the hearty singing, the music of the bands, the jingling tambourines, and yet— as General Arnold Brown points out in his history of Army work in Canada—'He was the Army. He had its spirit. It surged in the heart

that beat under his worsted coat as he served in the dry-goods store; it
throbbed as he attended the church meetings which were nearest in
spirit and exercises to those of his own dear Army'.

When the series of revival meetings in which he had taken part
ended and the travelling campaigners had moved to another town,
Jack Addie and a zealous companion, Jim Cathcart, decided to
continue the good work by holding cottage prayer meetings.

One night a stranger attended and when an opportunity was given
he stood and sang a Salvation Army song. Addie could hardly believe
his ears. 'Who are you, and where do you come from?' he asked
excitedly. The stranger identified himself as Joe Ludgate, a
Salvationist convert from England. Addie burst out: 'You are the
fellow I have been looking for during the past six months'.

'And you', replied Ludgate, 'are the fellow I have been trying to
find for six months'.

There and then, after reviving memories of experiences in
England, they resolved, by God's help, to plant the seed of their
beloved Salvation Army in Canada. The first open-air meeting was led
by the two pioneers in Victoria Park, London, on Sunday, 21 May
1882. Addie and Ludgate wore uniform similar to that of English
policemen. On their helmets were Salvation Army shields, below
which were inscribed the words, 'Prepare to meet thy God!'

It is recorded that the first song used on that historic occasion was
'We're travelling home to heaven above', with the recurring question,
'Will you go?' Could it possibly have been 'We're bound for the land
of the pure and the holy'? Both songs contain the same glorious
invitation anyway.

Jack Addie was a gifted soloist. It is said that from the day he set
foot in the Land of the Maple Leaf he was like an uncaged canary
bursting with song. When he arrived he sent to International
Headquarters for a song book and a red band for his cap. His was a
'religion of laughter', he wrote hundreds of songs and some years after
hoisting the flag in Canada was transferred to the United States, where
he went on singing, writing and preaching.

Joe Ludgate, too, was musical. He is reputed to have had a
pleasing voice and personality and to have been the first officer to use
the concertina in Canada. He wrote the words of many songs. He
reached the rank of Major and later became a minister in the USA,
serving as a chaplain to the US Army during the 1st World War.

The large-scale arrival of immigrants in Canada in the early years of
the century did much to launch the coast-to-coast formation of
songster brigades. Most of the Salvationist settlers were experienced
bandsmen and songsters from the Old Country who brought technical

ability and enthusiasm. The established English pattern began to take shape across the Dominion and, in place of the isolated groups of small vocal groups, the orthodox uniformed official sections grew up.

The year 1907 saw the beginning of the brigade at Peterborough, Ontario. Progress in all aspects of the songsters' service was rapid. In 1911 the Commanding Officer, Ensign Fred Merrett, reported that the brigade was 'one of the best' in Canada and gave the additional information: 'The uniform of the sisters comprises regulation hats, red waist coats trimmed with black braid and harp, and blue skirts, in which the brigade looks very neat indeed. The brothers, most of whom are bandsmen, also wear the regulation harp'.

The careful attention to smartness survived the formative years, for in 1939 a published report stated that the members of the brigade wore silk cords on festival occasions.

This brigade's soulful singing became a byword among Salvationists in Canada and never failed to charm and bless international visitors. Much of the success is due to the high standard demanded from Songster Leader Ben Smith, who was in charge for more than forty years.

Although a Toronto Divisional Songster Brigade was reported as being in action in 1910, it was not until the following year that corps activity in the 'Queen City' came to light. The songster brigade at Lisgar Street, twenty-eight strong, made its first appearance in the summer of 1911, becoming the forerunner of such sections as Earlscourt, West Toronto, East Toronto, Dovercourt and Toronto Temple.

The noted Danforth Songster Brigade was formed in 1914 and has had only three leaders—Wilfred Creighton, Lieut.-Colonel Alfred Keith and Eric Sharp, who has been in charge for nearly thirty-five years.

In 1959 the brigade toured in Great Britain and took part in the Songster Leaders' Councils Festival at the Royal Albert Hall. It thus became the first vocal group from beyond Europe to visit the Army's homeland. Six years later, further history was made when the songsters conducted their first campaign in Western Canada. This lasted ten days and extended as far as Vancouver.

In 1964 the then Territorial Commander, Commissioner Wycliffe Booth, presented the Songster Leader with the Certificate of Recognition for exceptional service.

Now the Agincourt Temple Songster Brigade, this fine section was selected to represent Canada at the International Congress 1978.

Beginnings at North Toronto came much later, but with the development of this suburban corps as a headquarters centre came the foundation of good musical sections. With the opening of doors of opportunity for broadcasting, the songster brigade at North Toronto pioneered a ministry which many other territories have been happy to follow.

In 1949 the songsters, under the leadership of Ernest Cunningham, participated in the USA Central Territory's music congress in Chicago and since then, in keeping with other Canadian brigades, has frequently crossed the border to conduct week-end meetings in the States.

With the increased opportunities for evangelical broadcasting a group of Toronto songsters was formed and conducted by the then Major Arnold Brown. This led to the launching of the regular weekly feature, 'This is my story', a half-hour programme which ran for many years and reached from Bermuda to the Yukon in the distant west.

Later came the popular television series, 'The living word', which was shown throughout the North American continent. Major (now General) Brown was again the mastermind behind this feature, for which the story-teller, linkman and vocal soloist was Lieut.-Colonel (then Captain) Ernest Miller, of Chicago. Colonel Bramwell Coles, who retired to Canada in 1952, gave considerable musical assistance to both features.

The year 1911 marked the foundation of the Winnipeg Citadel Songster Brigade. 'All wear regulation songster uniform', reported Lieut.-Colonel Joseph Pugmire soon after the formation, 'and they are not allowed to sing if dressed otherwise'.

Thus in the very beginning, guidelines of discipline were laid down and this, with good sound basic training, helped this brigade to become one of the best in Canada. The first leader was Brother Fred Wells, who hailed from Chippenham, England, to which corps he later returned to complete a long record of Army musical leadership.

The arrival in the corps of the talented Merritt family from Petersfield, England, meant an influx of voices that aided the building up of the section.

The *Empress of Ireland* disaster in the St Lawrence River whilst transporting Canadian delegates to the 1914 International Congress, seriously affected the Army's musical life of the territory. All but a handful of the staff band lost their lives and many of the territory's leading officers were among the victims.

Within a few months, however, the Canadian Staff Songsters were formed with Lieut.-Colonel Arthur Smeeton as leader and Major William Arnold as conductor. The brigade soon reached a high degree of proficiency and was in great demand throughout the territory.

Among the members were Captain Satya Mapp (who afterwards

became Mrs Lieut.-Commissioner Thomas Laurie), Captain Alfred Keith (a survivor of the *Empress* tragedy), Captain George Carter (who in 1921 became the fourth editor of *The Bandsman and Songster*), Ensign Ernest Pugmire (an *Empress* survivor) and Lieutenant Bert Greenaway (another survivor). The leader, Major Arnold, 'on loan' from the USA, like Ensign Pugmire, became a Commissioner and territorial leader.

The songsters' first appointment was at the welcome to the new Territorial Commander (Commissioner William J. Richards) and Mrs Richards. The meeting took place in the Massey Hall.

Later that year (1915) the new Western Canada Territory was inaugurated with headquarters in Winnipeg. This set-up demanded a transfer of personnel from Toronto and, as a result, the staff songsters, who showed such promise and seemed set for a long and useful ministry, ceased to function. But not at first. A photograph published in 1916 shows an almost different brigade, but Captain William Dray, in 1957 to become General Wilfred Kitching's Chief of the Staff, is easily recognized, squatting with crossed legs on the ground in the forefront of the picture, as was customary in those days.

Years afterwards, in 1969, another staff band was born under the leadership of the Territorial Music Secretary, Major Norman Bearcroft. It had taken fifty-four years for approval for such a revival. But the brave attempt to get the staff songsters going in 1914 cannot be forgotten.

Canada's first Festival of Song was held in 1953. This was intended to be the vocal partner of the annual Spring Festival which has for so long proved an instrumental feast. Brigades from Peterborough, London 1, Danforth, Dovercourt and Earlscourt gave solo items and sang as a massed chorus.

United singing did not come quickly in Canada, and for a long time this feature was not popular. The introduction of a series of Festivals of Gospel Song by Major Bearcroft, based upon the familiar British pattern, did much to break down the seeming prejudice and proved a distinct success, some of the programmes being recorded.

CHAPTER NINE

AUSTRALASIAN SAGA

WHEN Captain and Mrs Thomas Sutherland arrived in Adelaide in February 1881 to pioneer Salvation Army work in Australia they found an army of sixty-eight singing Salvationists waiting for them. They had enlisted under the flag since Edward Saunders and John Gore, both converted in Christian Mission meetings in England, had first held gatherings in the Labour League Hall in Adelaide.

It was Captain and Mrs Sutherland who later commenced Army work in Sydney, New South Wales, assisted by Captain Alexander Canty and Sister Mary Ann Cox. A trumpet call from the Captain's pocket cornet attracted the attention of the crowd gathered at Paddy's Market, and the first open-air meeting began with 'We're a band that shall conquer the foe'. The men played instruments; the women sang and beat tambourines.

The term 'singing company' seems to have been used in the Australia Eastern Territory from the earliest days. This should not be confused with the name of the young people's vocal sections now so popular throughout the Army world.

A *War Cry* report of January 1899 refers to the Christmas caroling activities of Paddington (Queensland) Singing Company. The context makes it clear that this was composed of adults. It is obvious from contemporary press cuttings that such companies were active in many corps. 'Singing companies' were still being formed as late as April 1908.

The first mention of 'songsters', at Broken Hill, appeared early in 1908, but there is no reference to a songster brigade or songster leader. Early in 1909 the official term seems to have come into vogue, but it is certain that singing brigades, by whatever title, were in existence much earlier, and that the leading songster brigades in the Eastern Territory date their foundations from long before 1910 when the Territorial Commander (Commissioner James Hay) introduced history books into corps life.

In 1922 a Territorial Headquarters Staff Songster Brigade was formed with Staff-Captain Gray as conductor and Brigadier (later Commissioner) John Lewis as leader. How long this section existed is not known, but in 1956 Territorial Salvation Singers were formed under the leadership of Mrs Stuart Peterson.

This efficient group was made up of female voices and set an example in equal part singing that many groups sought to emulate. The leader was promoted to Glory in 1959.

For the 1978 International Congress a divisional songster brigade from the territorial centre, to be known as the Sydney Salvation Singers, was invited to represent the vocal activities of Australasia.

In the Southern Territory singing groups appear to have been better organized. Within a short time of the beginning of Army work in Melbourne musical 'companies' were formed to travel the country, producing music 'shows' both for evangelism and also to raise money to wipe out debts.

The War Cry of 1888 records the activities of the Western and Eastern Musical Companies in Victoria. A report of September of that year shows the Eastern Company at Prahran: 'The bandsmen wore red jackets and the musical company red sashes . . . altogether it was a profitable time; salvation from first to last. The people gave liberally. I heard from good authority that they realized about thirty pounds to wipe out the debt.'

The Western Musical Company travelled from country town to country town, visiting Chinese camps (whose occupants had flooded into Australia for the gold rush), and had great success, 'tears flowing copiously as they sang most touching songs'.

There was usually a small band, a fiddler and guitarist in attendance, and the 'concert'—as it was always billed—concluded with a prayer meeting, seekers and 'bucketsful of glory'. These companies were described as 'the debt extinguishers'.

Among such companies were the Beulah Choralists of Queensland. A group of fifteen people, the choralists were formed as a touring company to help the Self-Denial Appeal. A string band, brass instruments and mouth organ were used for accompaniment purposes and the effect was said to be 'electrifying'.

The Government supplied the group with a steamer on two occasions so that a visit could be made to elderly people living at Dunwich. The choralists were active in 1893.

The success of these companies, and the exploits of the travelling brigades of salvation songsters in England, could have inspired Commandant Herbert Booth, in 1900, to form a Territorial Choir. This, organized by Major Holdaway under the Commandant's guidance, was formed to give assistance at the Brighton camp meetings, introduced by Herbert Booth when he became Territorial Commander.

So successful was the venture that the brigade took part in a number of Melbourne congresses and paved the way for the dispatch of the Federal Choralists for a tour through West and South Australia to raise funds for the new training college scheme.

In 1911 Commissioner Hay inaugurated the Territorial Staff Songsters with Lieut.-Colonel Ernest Knight as leader and conductor. This brigade gave valued service over a period of many years, but was never reinstituted.

Much later, in 1957, the Eastern Victoria Girls' Chorus was formed to take part in annual youth councils. The leader was Divisional Songster Leader Victor Rackham. So successful was the experiment that the chorus came into permanent use, giving radio programmes and appearing on television. Songster Leader Rackham led the efficient Hawthorn Songster Brigade for some years.

The first corps songster brigade in the Southern Territory is said to have been formed at Adelaide, scene of the pioneer venture of Saunders and Gore. A date given is 1902, but a singing brigade could have been functioning there and elsewhere long before.

In 1959 a brigade from Western Australia visited the Eastern States for the first time. Perth Fortress Songster Brigade, led by Allan Pengilly, a noted composer of vocal music, travelled a distance of 4,400 miles to carry out a week-end campaign. En route for Melbourne the brigade stopped at Adelaide Congress Hall, Norwood and Ballaret (where a broadcast programme was given). Festivals were presented at Hawthorn, Melbourne Temple, Box Hill and Brunswick.

When Captain George Pollard and Lieutenant Edward Wright farewelled from the Exeter Hall, London, to open the work in New Zealand in 1883, their faith was high. So high that they declared that they meant to go through New Zealand till everybody was saved, and then would return to headquarters for fresh instructions!

Failure to achieve this ambition was certainly not due to lack of enthusiasm. Every possible device was used with remarkable success. Both young men realized the power of song to influence the decision of hesitant hearers and the early Army compositions swept across the 'land of the long white cloud' with telling results.

One of the first songster brigades was formed at Wellington Citadel in 1913 and has a continuous record of service to its credit. Songster Leader Ray Atherford was in charge for some years. Over a period the brigade has made regular television appearances, sometimes in conjunction with a Salvationist lightning artist, Maitland Ramage.

Auckland Congress Hall Songster Brigade is another well-known vocal section. Thomas Rive, distinguished Salvationist composer, was the leader of the brigade for some time.

The songsters made their first television appearance in 1966 when,

South Africa

Singing brigades of one kind or another came into being in South Africa soon after the beginnings of the work there, but it was not until 1915 that a section was commissioned in Cape Town, the pioneering city.

The songster brigade at Cape Town 1 was formed by Mrs Adjutant Herbert Hodgson. Since its inception the brigade, in the nature of things, has always had a floating membership. Commenced when the corps was closely allied to Territorial Headquarters, of which building the corps hall was a part, the pioneer members were officers or from officers' families.

This meant that, when the territorial centre was moved to Johannesburg in 1924, some of the stalwarts were sadly missed. But the brigade continued as a vital force and has a creditable record of service.

Leaders of the past include Lieut.-Colonel Leslie Pender who, with Mrs Pender, farewelled from the corps to enter the International Training College in 1931 and never returned to serve in South Africa; Captain Nell Clark, daughter of the well-known missionary, Colonel Fred Clark; and Songster Leader Dorothy Joy, who was in charge during the time her father, Colonel Edward Joy, was Editor of the South African *War Cry*.

The first accompaniments were provided by Songster Secretary (later Adjutant) Anne Rauch at the piano, and among early organists was Mrs Fred Dalziel, a daughter of Commissioner and Mrs Robert Hoggard. With her husband, a member of a noted Army musical family, Mrs Dalziel later returned to England and served in a similar capacity with Wood Green Songsters for some years. Commissioner Hesketh King was a member of the brigade for some time.

With the transfer of Territorial Headquarters to Johannesburg the musical interests of Salvationists in that city took on a new lease of life. Officers of several nationalities brought with them valued vocal experience gained in their homelands and in Cape Town. This resulted in an upsurge of enthusiasm and the founding of Johannesburg City Songster Brigade and other such groups in the vicinity.

Later came the introduction of African brigades. Wisely these sections, whilst seeking to retain the typical Army Western outlook on gospel singing, did not entirely abandon the traditional vocal prowess of their fathers.

Few African Salvationists sing from old notation; they are more acquainted with tonic sol-fa. When, in 1955, General Wilfred Kitching returned from his first campaign in Africa he was full of praise for excellent national singing groups he had heard. When pressed by an Army editor to give the reason for his unqualified tributes, he said the outstanding features were precision, memorizing of parts and words, excellent response to the leader and light and shade. For good measure he added: 'Far exceeding the average brigade in this country'.

Johannesburg Central Songster Brigade, consisting of Africans, made a marked impression upon its audiences when it took part in a Bantu Congress held in 1957. Singing without musical accompaniment, the songsters sang from the Bantu Song Book in Zulu and added their own harmonies.

Another brigade that has sprung into prominence recently is that attached to the Central Division. This, with Soweto as its centre, was formed to participate in the International Congress 1978. The nucleus of the group are members of the songster brigade regularly functioning in the Soweto township.

Despite ever-recurring violence and political upheaval, of which the world is well aware, Salvationists in this community are maintaining their consistent witness, and the dedicated services of the singing evangelists are making a vital contribution.

Durban Central Corps was opened by Commissioner James Hay in 1923. When the songster brigade was first formed is not clear, but its modern history dates from the summer of 1929 when the section was reconstituted by Ensign (later Lieut.-Colonel) Herbert Wood, now living in retirement in Toronto. The Colonel served for some years as Editor of the South African *War Cry* and his last appointment was Editor-in-Chief in Canada.

The brigade has farewelled many songsters for the training college over the years and is still a distinct asset to corps life in this South African beauty spot and portside city.

Another small but efficient brigade with an impressive record is Pretoria. Again many nationalities combined to bring this section into being and tribute is paid to the encouragement given by Adjutant (later Lieut.-Colonel) and Mrs Fred Rout when they were stationed in the town in a social services appointment. The Colonel acted as leader for some time.

Songsters in South Africa, like those in Rhodesia, have benefited from the recent visits of Colonel Bernard Adams and Major Leslie Condon from the international centre.

Rhodesia

When Major and Mrs John Pascoe and their pioneer party arrived at Fort Salisbury, Mashonaland, after a six-month, thousand-mile journey from Kimberley, Cecil Rhodes was there to meet them. He promised that a farm and two areas of land for building purposes would be reserved for the Army's use.

That was in 1891. A year later the promise was fulfilled and a barracks and farm of 3,000 acres in the Mazoe Valley was handed over. The farm was named 'Pearson', after Colonel William Pearson, who had recently been promoted to Glory.

Ten years earlier, Pearson, the Army's first song-writer seer, had declared:

> We're marching on to conquer all,
> Before our God the world shall fall;
> We'll face the foe, to battle go,
> And never, never run away.

This determination has been reflected in the lives and service of white and black officers in Rhodesia, and with the emergence of national leaders the work has continued in the face of war, murder, uprisings and political problems yet to be solved.

Music-making among the white populace has been centred upon Salisbury. Because of the transfer of many British Salvationists, some of them for limited periods, the English style of songster activity has been maintained over many years. These comrades have added lustre to the long list of songster leaders who have inspired the Salisbury City Songsters.

One such leader was James McHarg, who hailed from Ayr, in Scotland. Holding the qualifications of MA and LRAM (teacher of singing), he placed his wealth of knowledge and experience of the vocal art at the disposal of the songsters of Rhodesia and served in several local officer appointments after settling in Salisbury some forty years ago.

In the township of Harare, an African songster brigade has been in existence for many years and a similar hard-working section is part of the busy corps programme at Mitanda, some thirty miles from Salisbury. The songsters' uniforms incorporate the harp design which was popular in the Western world some years ago, and a bright red and blue sash, embroidered in white with the name of the corps.

The famous Howard Institute, by virtue of its history of educational development, has become a centre of Army singing. Several former students, instilled with enthusiasm for the Christian vocal art, have taken up Army section leadership in Rhodesia.

Zambia

In what used to be known as Northern Rhodesia, organized vocal groups are not plentiful, but some brigades are active.

The musical life of the command is centred at the Chikankata Institute. The school song, set to music by Brigadier Laura Dutton, who gave so many years to Army service in Rhodesia and Zambia before retiring from active service in 1977, graphically describes the setting and highlights the objectives.

> With God's green hills around us,
>   And rivers running by,
> Our school is set in a goodly place,
>   'Neath the blue of Afric's sky.
> We've come to Chikankata to learn of many things,
>   To grow in grace and take our place
>   As citizens of our land.
>
> We belong to Chikankata,
>   And we're proud of our school,
> We learn to play—and sing and pray
>   As each day newly dawns.
> God bless our school and help us all
>   To work with heart and hand;
> United in our aim to build
>   A happy Christian land.

The song was sung for the first time at the graduation ceremony in 1959.

The institute at Chikankata is adjacent to the hospital and leprosy settlement. It consists of a boarding school, a two-year teacher training course, a two-year domestic science course for girls and a three-year trades course (carpentry and building) for boys. This makes a 'family' of some 400.

Many of the African songs sung at the institute are passed on from generation to generation. They have not yet been written down. In the school singing lessons the younger children are taught the songs of their ancestors by the African members of the staff. The older students enjoy learning English folk-songs.

Four-part harmony comes naturally to the students, but it is not western harmony. They do not sing the accidentals, and this technique clothes the singing with its own beauty. Salvation Army songs are learned with equal enthusiasm and the choir's activity at Christmas and Easter has become an integral part of the curriculum.

Easter Sunday is really special. Early in the morning everyone gathers at the top of the hill overlooking Chikankata for the sunrise service, and as they march the strains of the chorus, 'He lives, I know He lives', can be heard, increasing in volume as the students are joined by the officers and nurses from the hospital and finally those of the leprosy patients who are well enough to join.

Zaïre

In the first Salvation Army open-air meeting held in Zaïre (then the Belgian Congo) in 1934 the pioneer, Adjutant Henri Becquet, sang 'We have a message, a message from Jesus'. Singing in French, the Adjutant changed the first word to the singular personal pronoun to give more power to that initial witness. Mrs Becquet accompanied at a small portable organ.

The organ, twenty-eight years before, lay forlorn and forgotten in a second-hand shop of a little English country town when it was noticed by a Salvation Army Captain in charge of the local corps. How much did the shopkeeper want for it? Thirty shillings? He bought it.

The Captain's wife was something of an organist herself, and the instrument began its useful revived life as it moved from corps to corps in the British Territory.

When the officers, Adjutant (later Lieut.-Colonel) and Mrs Bertie Rolls, were stationed at Bolton, in Lancashire, Captain Henri Becquet was appointed to assist them. The Captain was a gifted musician, excelling as a violinist and becoming one of the family. When Captain Becquet left the Rolls's quarters to take over his first command, the little harmonium went with him, a gift of love from the family. It remained with the future Commissioner and Mrs Becquet in their appointments in France and Belgium and accompanied them on their pioneering work in Zaïre.

Mrs Becquet, now living in retirement in Belgium and one of the first officers in that command to denote her intention of being in London for the International Congress 1978, remembers that first open-air meeting and the indoor service that followed.

'It was difficult to find out from where the men or the women's voices rose', she says. 'When the melody reached too high a pitch the women quickly dropped suddenly to the lower octave'. But, she explains, that was more than forty years ago, and African children of today receive training much earlier than their forebears.

From this humble beginning groups of singers were formed in nearly every Army centre in the territory, some blossoming into efficient songster brigades—such as that at Kinshasa, formerly Leopoldville, where the attendance at Sunday morning holiness meetings often reaches 1,000.

Congo

Requested by General Edward Higgins to open Army work in the French Congo, later known as Equatorial Africa, Adjutant and Mrs Becquet, with a number of officers, a flag and a band, crossed the

Congo river in March 1937 to hold a meeting at Brazzaville. This was then a part of the Belgian Congo Territory but became a separate command in 1953.

The Salvationists sang as they sailed, the little band accompanying them, and Captain and Mrs Marcel Beney, sent on in advance to prepare the way, were at the dockside to welcome the 'invaders'.

Nigeria

In how many countries that redoubtable warrior, George Scott Railton, had a hand in starting Army work, directly or indirectly, is difficult to say. Some of them have been named in this history. More will surely come.

Railton visited West Africa in 1903 and, never lacking initiative, taught a group of village boys to sing, 'We must all be soldiers in the Army of the Lord', to the tune of 'John Brown's body', clapping their hands as they did so. He wrote, 'Each day has strengthened my conviction that proper praying, fighting Salvationists can be certain of gaining a sure foothold among these warm-hearted people.'

The true internationalism of the Army was revealed when Commissioner Henry Bullard, then Territorial Commander in the West Indies, heard of the possibilities of officially opening the work in Nigeria and offered a dozen of his officers—great-grandchildren of West Africans who had been shipped across the Atlantic as slaves—to assist Lieut.-Colonel and Mrs George Souter in their pioneering. That was in 1920.

Lagos Central Songster Brigade has for years featured as a European-style vocal group. It was a proud moment for the songsters when, in 1958, a new organ and banner were dedicated by the General Secretary, Brigadier F. Kevin Munn. The organ had been donated by the USA Central Territory and was presented to Songster Leader Kenneth Edwards some weeks previously at his home corps, Regent Hall.

The songster leader was due to return to Nigeria for a further term of Government service and the organ travelled with him. He is now the leader of an efficient brigade at Rushden, in the Midlands of England.

Songster endeavours in Nigeria are by no means confined to verse and chorus contributions. Africans and European singers happily unite without the semblance of an embarrassing colour bar. General Frederick Coutts remembers one such occasion when, in the First Baptist Church in Lagos, a combined brigade surprised a congregation of more than 600 people with 'The Awakeners', with the General Secretary, Lieut.-Colonel Haakon Dahlstrøm, at the piano.

Ghana

Salvationists of West Africa owe a tremendous debt to the inspiration and enthusiasm of Colonel William Fleming who, before his promotion to Glory in 1973, was Ghana's Officer Commanding.

The Colonel's rugged, hearty salvationism made its own appeal and his love for music and song encouraged the formation of sections in the most remote outposts as well as in the large towns and cities.

The beginnings of work in the Gold Coast, as it was called, had an indirect musical genesis. A visitor from there, on a business trip to London, was attracted by singing in the street. He discovered the sound to come from an Army open-air meeting, attended a meeting at Clapton Congress Hall and became converted.

Anxious for the work to start in his country he sought an interview with General Bramwell Booth, offered to pay for his officership training, as proof of his sincerity, and to pay his own fare back to Accra.

In 1922 King Hudson was commissioned a Lieutenant and appointed to 'open fire' in his own town of Duakwa.

The Ghana Territory holds an annual singing rally, and brigades, commissioned songsters and unofficial sections travel many miles to take part.

It is all something of a miracle. In the heart of any African bush will be found a singing brigade, all the vocal work usually unaccompanied. The leader invariably hums the first line to set the key. Where he gets his pitch from remains a mystery, for he seems to carry no tuning fork or other device.

Perhaps part of the answer is in the hearts as well as the heads of African Salvationists. That is harmony that transcends tribal hatred and long-standing racial feuds, and reaches its most glorious cadence when a congregation in West Africa lifts its voice as well as its eyes to sing 'Guide me, O Thou great Jehovah' to the tune of 'Calabar'.

CHAPTER ELEVEN

VARIETY IN THE EAST

India

IT is not easy to imagine India as a land of song: plagues and famines; fever and sudden death through mysterious causes; floods and earthquakes—but rarely a nation of singers.

And yet man has always wanted to sing to express deep emotion. India is no exception. It is an enchanting land whose people continually engage in pagan festivals, singing their simple melodies, dancing in weird fascination, beating tom-toms with a persistence which eventually finds a rhythmic echo in the throbbing of pulses. The songs of nature, the music of the soul.

The Salvation Army's success in India has always been its observance of 'In Christ there is no East or West'. The art of tolerance was early learned and Army missionaries, without seeking to destroy the indigenous idiom, have rather sought to capture it and include it in the ministry of soul-saving and spiritual healing.

In 1912 Commissioner Frederick Booth-Tucker summed up the situation. 'Army music in India', he said, 'is largely vocal, and it is Indian, which explains much. There is little hope of teaching the elders to sing four-part harmony, for such a thing is not understood by them. We have to turn our attention to the children in our schools, where they are taught to sing in two parts.'

The first fruits of such teaching were seen and heard during the visit of King George V and Queen Mary to India in 1911 for the great Durbar celebrating His Majesty's Coronation. As the royal couple drove past, girls in the Army's care blended their well-trained soprano and contralto voices to sing 'God save the King'.

Times have changed and such sentiment may have faded, but the salvation song of India still has a resonant ring, and the message is the same.

In 1917 a territorial headquarters' songster brigade was formed in Bombay, and this became the forerunner of several such groups in all Indian territories. As in other parts of the mission field, European officers aided considerably in establishing the western style of presentation.

The songster brigade at Calcutta was formed in 1958 by Brigadier (later Commissioner) and Mrs Don Smith. These officers were instrumental in inaugurating many such brigades at corps with which they have been associated in different parts of the world. Mrs Smith was pianist for the Norwegian Staff Songsters before entering the training college.

The first Indian to become a Territorial Commander was Commissioner Narayana Muthiah, who was promoted to Glory in 1959. In his younger days he was noted as an effective singing evangelist. With the aid of a native guitar he sang soulfully in Tamil.

Commissioner Muthiah was always linked with the prayer song, 'O Jesus come Thou to pour on us the spirit of prayer', familiar in all Indian territories. Colonel Musa Bhai, who commanded the Southern India Territory from 1896 to 1898, after walking from village to village conducting meetings, would seek the help of the young Captain Muthiah to massage his weary feet.

On one such occasion the Captain began to sing a certain Tamil melody which brought immediate inspiration to the Colonel. He began to dictate the words forming in his mind and the Captain wrote them down. The prayer song, a favourite in officers' meetings since that time, is still found in the Tamil song book.

Incidentally, while the one who wrote down the words became the first Indian territorial commander, the one who dictated them became the first Indian Commissioner.

Any musical history which the Pakistan Territory has can date only from 1948 when the countries were separated. For some years prior to this a songster brigade had been functioning at Lahore Central Hall.

The songster leader at the time of its formation was Major (later Colonel) Charles Green, and other foundation members were Commissioner Carl Richards and Colonel and Mrs Edward Sheard.

Sri Lanka

Sri Lanka's most famous Salvationist son was Arnolis Weerasooriya. It is not recorded that he had any great musical gifts or wrote any songs, but there is musical 'feel' in his entrancing name. Even to repeat the name half aloud sends the five syllables into rhythmic patterns of sweetly flowing melody.

This young Sinhalese belonged to one of the leading families of Southern Ceylon. He was a teacher and already a Christian when he first met the Army. The preaching may have attracted him. It could have been the singing. These both could have been contributory factors. We do know, however, that it was the fact that the pioneer officer, Captain Wallace Gladwin, was prepared to live as a Sinhalese and to adopt native dress that decided Arnolis to become a Salvationist.

Weerasooriya was trained for officership in the newly-opened training college at Madras and assisted Tucker in great revival meetings in Gujerat. He accompanied the Indian contingent to the first International Congress in 1886, at which his lilting name was on everyone's lips and he was a popular figure.

It has always been difficult to maintain singing brigades of an orthodox character in Sri Lanka because of a lack of permanent leadership. European officers have from time to time been responsible for an upsurge of interest, and in this respect the name of Lieut.-Colonel George Lovegrove, now living in retirement in the USA, must be remembered. Bands and songster brigades on the lovely island are grateful to him.

After the 2nd World War the songster brigade at Colombo was re-formed and continues to give appreciated service, delighting in providing excellent musical support to visiting international leaders.

Singapore and Malaysia

It was that man Railton again. In the early days of the century he reconnoitred for God and the Army in Singapore, leaving an imprint of salvationism with the memory of the uniform and a small Gladstone bag.

General Bramwell Booth stopped there in 1926 on his way to the Far East, and nine years later Brigadier (later Commissioner) and Mrs Herbert Lord arrived to pioneer Army work. The Brigadier had been a songster in Cambridge, England, before becoming an officer and had memorized countless songs, which habit was to come to his rescue time and time again during subsequent internment in the 2nd World War and the Korean War.

There was hardly a chance for singing brigades to be officially organized, for in a few brief years the new command was caught up in the vortex of world conflict. The Brigadier, his General Secretary (Major Charles Davidson), Adjutant Fred Harvey and Captain Stanley Cottrill, the present Chief of the Staff, were interned for the duration and the promising work was throttled almost at birth.

This was but a temporary setback and when peace returned the activity soon got into its stride. Although there is not much songster brigade history, singing has taken its place beside preaching the gospel and progressive social service in establishing Army work in this area.

Indonesia

Officers of many nationalities have helped to make the history of Army music in Indonesia. Colonel and Mrs William Harris, as young officers in the early 1920's, took their enthusiasm and English background to Java where a songster brigade was formed.

The name of Lieut.-Colonel Leonard Woodward will always be linked with Celebes. His inventive construction of flute bands has already been told. It did not take long, at the beginning of missionary service, to realize that the Salvationists of Celebes were enthusiastic singers.

In the Colonel's early days as a divisional commander, a national officer, visiting his quarters, heard a recording of 'Abide with me'. It was the first time he had seen or listened to a gramophone, and as he listened to the grand old hymn, which he had not heard before, he made hurried caligraphic signs while the record played.

Later, when the divisional commander visited the officer's corps he was treated to a rendering by the songster brigade of the hymn. It was sung in four-part harmony which corresponded identically with the recorded version.

Most corps in Indonesia have a songster brigade, some more than one. The corps officer is normally the leader.

Some twenty-five years ago an Army leader, with his wife, visited an Army hospital at Pelantungan where a choir of leprosy patients was gathered to sing to the distinguished guests. A programme was presented. Most of the songs were enjoyed, but when 'Jerusalem, my happy home' was sung the visitors were deeply moved. Many of the young people bore the marks of the dreaded disease upon them.

The leaders, with tears trickling down their cheeks, were more distressed than the singers. The majority of them wore white uniforms, and although some were blind because of advanced stages of the malady, they all held their heads high and faced toward the heavens, trying, it seemed, to get the battlements of the New Jerusalem in focus.

That kind of Army vocal music merits a place in this history.

The Philippines

When Colonel and Mrs Alfred Lindvall farewelled from London to commence Army work in the Philippines, they received from General Evangeline Booth a flag bearing the inscription, 'The Philippine Islands for Christ'. These officers, who had already given thirty-six years' service in South America and Brazil, arrived in Manila on 23 May 1937.

Despite the claim that the Philippines is the one Christian nation in the Far East, a footing was not easy to secure. After four halls had been hired, the pioneers ventured forth to hold open-air meetings. People were attracted and crowds gathered to listen.

Within six months police intervened. Singing was prohibited and a ruling made that Army meetings must be confined to indoors. Not lacking in resourcefulness the leaders immediately realized that the whole of one side of one of the halls could be opened on to the busy thoroughfare which ran alongside. Full advantage of this was taken and passers-by continued to congregate to hear the happy singing and the gospel message.

When the police arrived the Colonel pointed out that they were not holding an open-air meeting, and were complying with the instructions. The police were adamant that the Salvationists were holding up the traffic. People were stopping to listen and blocking up the street.

The Colonel calmly expressed the opinion that this was a matter for the police and not The Salvation Army, whereupon the impatient officer of the law moved the crowd on—into the Army hall! There were many seekers that night.

The training of officers in the Philippines commenced in 1938. The ten cadets were formed into a singing group and became pioneer music makers in the command. Early copies of *The War Cry*, printed in four languages, give the information that toward the end of that year a Luzon divisional quartet came into being, composed of a Filipino officer and candidate, and an overseas officer couple. They were featured in broadcasts in 1939.

October 1954 saw the commissioning of two songster brigades, at Baguio (Northern Luzon) and La Paz Illoilo (Panay Island). At the time of writing only five of the twenty-six corps have a commissioned songster brigade, but because of the Filipinos' inherent love for music and their ability to harmonize, almost every corps has a singing group which gives adequate and faithful support to the meeting.

Hong Kong

In contrast to so many other countries where The Salvation Army was unwanted and unwelcomed, work in Hong Kong began, in 1930, in response to a government request for a home for women and girls to be opened. The inauguration of two corps quickly followed, one at Kowloon and the other on Hong Kong island.

At first the work was directed from Peking, but then came under the direction of the newly-formed South China Command. When Brigadier and Mrs James Sansom arrived to lead the forces of the new command the hopes of the musicians ran high. The Brigadier was a former member of the International Staff Band and an able vocal soloist. His earliest campaigns in his new appointment included plenty of infectious singing and he had plans for a large-scale development of vocal activity, but within a matter of months he was promoted to Glory, at the height of his considerable powers.

At this time (1936) some commissioned songster brigades were active in corps at Canton, China, but there were no official vocal sections in Hong Kong until the work was revived after the 2nd World War. Among Royal Air Force personnel who arrived to occupy Hong Kong in September 1945 were seven Salvationists.

In the YMCA building they met for a meeting led by Lieut.-Colonel William Darby, then Officer Commanding South China, and were joined by Major (later Lieut.-Colonel) and Mrs Harold Littler, who with their children had just been released from internment. On the following Sunday the servicemen attended meetings at Kowloon Central Corps and, although no brass instruments were available, formed themselves into a male voice party to add blessing to the gatherings and bring encouragement to their Chinese comrades.

The first songster brigade was commissioned at Wanchai and the second, in 1952, at Kowloon Central Corps.

In October 1965 work was re-established in Taiwan by retired Colonel and Mrs George Lancashire and Army activity on this island has now been amalgamated with that in Hong Kong.

Korea

The Army's first General had a flair for the spectacular. At a Crystal Palace day in 1908 that marked the Movement's forty-third anniversary, Colonel and Mrs Robert Hoggard were dedicated to Korea. It greatly cheered William Booth's heart that, at long last, the way had been opened for the work to commence there.

True to form, Railton had been there already, this time with Commissioner John Lawley, the General's faithful henchman for so long. Government officials were interviewed and permission was granted.

In the Hoggards' pioneering party was Captain Margaret Newnham, a daughter of John Newnham who was a clarinet player in the early days of the International Staff Band. The Captain had a musical ear and gave great support to the leaders in those first meetings.

Among reinforcements sent to help were Captain Herbert Lord and Captain Charles Sylvester. Both became members of Korea's first brass band and Captain Newnham became Mrs Lord.

A territorial headquarters songster brigade in Seoul was formed in 1937, when Commissioner Thomas Wilson was the Territorial

Commander. This was a truly international group, its members coming from Switzerland, Sweden, England, Australia, Canada and Japan, as well as Korea.

In more recent times songster brigades in this territory have been mostly composed of students and youthful workers. The voices are well balanced and well trained. The result is generally pleasing and tuneful.

This is something of an achievement when it is remembered that the traditional music of Korea is composed solely from a scale of five notes. Because of this there is to this day difficulties with accidentals, especially in congregational singing.

The efficient youthful vocalists of the territory will have their place in a later chapter.

Japan

A Japanese in the San Francisco training garrison in 1893 spent his spare time translating some 200 Army songs into Chinese and the language of his homeland. He had met the Army in that great American city and longed for the work to open up in Japan.

Later that year he travelled to place the needs of his country before General William Booth. The General did not forget the pleadings of this fine young convert from the Buddhist faith, for within eighteen months, after two leaders had been appointed and had to withdraw because of illness, Colonel and Mrs Edward Wright were chosen to be the pioneers in Japan.

The Colonel was the twenty-year-old Lieutenant who, with Captain George Pollard, had launched The Salvation Army in New Zealand by singing 'We're bound for the land of the pure and the holy' as they stood at the Dunedin Fountain.

The pioneers arrived wearing Japanese costume and that night, when walking through the European quarter of Tokyo, the Colonel passed a public-house in which a piano was being thumped as the accompaniment to a man's lusty voice. He was singing:

> The Salvation Army has come!
> The Salvation Army has come!
> O Lord have mercy upon us!
> The Salvation Army has come!

Another musical beginning!

When the Founder visited Tokyo in 1907 a singing brigade was formed to lead the congregational singing and this set a pattern for all territorial events.

In 1916, following the formation of the Territorial Staff Band on a permanent basis, a territorial songster brigade came into being and the inclusion of western officers with considerable vocal experience encouraged the Japanese singers and added strength and 'class' to their apologetic performances. Among these were such personalities as Major Ernest Pugmire, Staff-Captain Herbert Climpson and Captain Henry Pennick.

The year 1930 saw the arrival in Japan of Captain Charles Davidson, whose appointment as Private Secretary to the Territorial Commander, Commissioner Gunpei Yamamuro, brought him into immediate contact with the musicians of the territory. With a short break this gifted musician served in Japan until December 1964 when, as a Commissioner and the Territorial Commander, he was appointed to take charge of the New Zealand Territory.

In November 1957 a territorial staff songster brigade was formed with Captain (later Major) Chiyeko Mochimaru as leader and Captain William Banks as deputy leader. Commissioner Davidson served as pianist whenever he was available. Brigadier (later Colonel) Dorothy Phillips, an American officer, was the Executive Officer.

Within ten days of the first rehearsal the brigade took part in a holiness meeting conducted by the Territorial Commander at Kanda, singing 'Since Jesus came into my heart'. Shortly afterwards the brigade supported Colonel Yasowo Segawa when he gave a broadcast talk on the life of Commissioner Yamamuro.

In 1965 the memorable Centenary Service in Westminster Abbey concluded with the singing of Charles Coller's majestic song, a verse of which could prove a fitting ending to this survey of world-wide Army vocal music:

> Salvation! Sing salvation;
>   Was e'er so grand a theme?
> Sing on till every nation
>   Shall hear of Calvary's stream.
> Sing out the tidings glorious
>   That God so loved the world,
> Till Christ shall be victorious
>   And hell be backward hurled.

Dr Fulton's prophecy has come true. These people have sung their way round the world.

CHAPTER TWELVE

THEY SET THE PATTERN

International Staff Songsters

NO doubt inspired by the formation of the International Staff Band in 1891, a group of vocal enthusiasts a year later decided that a party drawn from one or two departments at International Headquarters could be well employed undertaking week-end specialing.

The then Adjutant Herbert Jackson was invited to be the leader and the young Salvationists accepted the opportunities presented and developed a real love for part-singing and campaigning. Many of them uttered their first platform discourses when serving in this way.

No great publicity was given to this venture, probably because the Founder's opinion of organized choirs was well known and had to be respected. But five years later, in March 1897, a Minute issued by the Chief of the Staff brought the International Staff Songsters into being, with Herbert Jackson as the leader and the original party forming the basis of the group.

The purposes of the new brigade were clearly stated. Each songster was expected to:

1. Spread salvation news.
2. Undertake engagements, as did the International Staff Band, on week-nights, and every third week to carry out a week-end campaign.
3. Be available for every engagement, the brigade's duties taking precedence over all other commitments.

The amazing thing is that William Booth permitted this section to be inaugurated a year *before* he gave authority to Commissioner John Carleton to form a corps songster brigade at Penge. Several reasons have been propounded over the years.

Some felt that the Founder, in his astute discernment, was prepared to allow the Staff Songsters to be 'guinea-pigs' in a good cause and that he, carefully observing the experiment, saw no reason why Carleton's request should not finally be granted. Others felt that Commissioner Carleton, after the establishment and initial success of the Staff Songsters, used this as an excuse for the experiment to be carried out at corps level. The fact that Jackson was a soldier of Penge Corps could have intensified Carleton's determination!

Another theory is that William Booth did not agree with the formation of the Staff Songsters and was never really converted to the idea of songster brigades as such. In other words, all this could have happened with his official permission but against his personal preference.

The fact is that this new expression of vocal interest at the Army's hub came into being in 1897 and gave thirty-one years of invaluable service, setting a standard of singing, deportment and Christian witness which inspired others and led to the formation of songster brigades.

Colonel Jackson, as he became, was a man of many gifts, which he was encouraged to develop to the full. As a man of business affairs he graced the accountancy profession with dignity and skill. As an evangelist his power of expression, persuasion and leadership drew many to high and holy service. As a musician and vocal conductor he became an outstanding figure.

For seven years the Colonel was assisted in the leadership by Lieut.-Colonel Albert Campion, and other early-day Staff Songsters' officials included Staff-Captain Richard Hughes and Adjutant (later Lieut.-Colonel) Cecil Rees, both of whom served as secretary.

Unlike the Staff Band, the Staff Songsters never had a permanent practice room. For mid-day rehearsals they were expected to gather wherever there happened to be space: in the basement of '101'; the boiler house; passageways; among the piled stocks in the stationery department; and latterly in the strong room of '107', the home of The Salvation Army Assurance Society until the blitz of 1941.

A feature of Sunday afternoon meetings almost from the brigade's inception was the presentation, 'Round the world in sixty minutes'. This consisted of carefully chosen songs from many countries, with the songsters dressing in national costumes to give correct interpretation to the colourful items. With the passing of time the Sunday afternoon programmes became longer, which meant a subtle change of title to 'Round the world in ninety minutes'!

In 1922, after twenty-five years as the leader, Colonel Jackson was appointed Chief Secretary in Switzerland and his successor as conductor was Staff-Captain (later Colonel) Railton Howard. At the same time Brigadier Herbert Colledge was announced to be the leader, thus following the pattern observed by the International Staff Band.

The Brigadier, who later became a Lieut.-Commissioner, had served in his homeland, Australia, and in India and New Zealand. He served as a chaplain to the Australian forces in Europe in the 1st World War. This joint arrangement did not last long and upon Brigadier Colledge's farewell from International Headquarters for an overseas appointment, Staff-Captain Howard assumed the double leadership role so successfully managed by his illustrious predecessor.

Railton Howard had been a member of the Brigade since 1901 and Colonel Jackson's deputy for ten years. He was the second son of Commissioner T. Henry Howard, then Chief of the Staff, and had already gained a well-deserved reputation as a conductor of vocal groups.

He was the leader of a singing group at New Barnet before a songster brigade was formed there; for two years he acted as songster leader at Clapton Congress Hall while Major Edith Rogers was ill; he formed the Harrow Songster Brigade in 1916 and remained its leader until 1953; and later was to become the conductor of the Assurance Songsters throughout its nearly thirty-years' history.

Although the honour of being the first leader of massed singing in the Army rightly belongs to Herbert Booth, with those mammoth white-sashed 'choirs' at the Crystal Palace, no one fostered the idea of united singing more than, or remained the undisputed monarch in the middle of such contingents as long as, Colonel Howard.

At the end of the 1st World War, the Divisional Commander for North London, Lieut.-Colonel (later Commissioner) George Langdon, asked the Colonel to form a divisional chorus of 100 voices to take part in a series of festivals. This he did, with remarkable results.

Throughout the 1920s and '30s and well into the '40s, Colonel Howard controlled large choruses at national events while National Bandmaster A. W. Punchard fulfilled a similar function with the bands. The Colonel's rhythmic, clenched-fisted swing of the arms became a familiar sight at Clapton Congress Hall, the Crystal Palace, Alexandra Palace, Royal Albert Hall, and many a town hall and concert auditorium up and down Britain.

Senior-Major Edward Saywell, as National Secretary for Bands and Songster Brigades, took over the role after the 2nd World War. Railton Howard has had his worthy successors, but he was the pioneer.

Mrs Howard was proud to tell that she was a Staff Songster before her husband. Together they served in this brigade, and in the Assurance Songsters and at Harrow. She was a great singing enthusiast.

During the whole of the Staff Songsters' existence practically all their travelling was done by train or, in the London area, by tram and bus. It was something of a leap forward, therefore, when the brigade, as *The Bandsman and Songster* for 2 October 1926 reported, journeyed to Tring by *charabanc*.

Special interest was added to the occasion by the presence in the festival of the Chief of the Staff and Mrs Commissioner Edward J. Higgins. Their daughter, Captain Ruth Higgins, was the Tring Commanding Officer.

A year later the brigade adopted a 'novel way' of travelling to Brighton for an engagement. The help of several friends who owned motor cars was enlisted and a convoy of vehicles made its unhurried way to the coast, each car flying an Army flag.

With the change in leadership in 1922 came a change of name. It was decided that the singers would henceforth be known as the International Headquarters Songster Brigade, coming into line with the official designation of the International Staff Band. But the members were still regarded as the Staff Songsters, and the 'tag' remained.

The Staff Songsters were blest with good accompanists. A portable organ was used, a measure of consistent tone being assured by systematic and controlled rapid pedalling. In the brigade's latter years it was well served by Dorothy Swinfin (Mrs Joseph Long), Percy McLean and others.

Soloists were in good supply. The names of Katie Mayers (Mrs Munro Laurie), Lily Mayers (Mrs Percy Berriss), Jean Laurie (Mrs Commissioner Charles Durman), the daughters of Major and Mrs John Hill (Ivy and Connie), Katie Chapman and Brigadier William Bedford are imperishable in the annals of this pioneer section. Colonel Howard himself featured 'The old drummer' on programmes with marked success.

Solos were generally sung with brigade accompaniment, and especially was this effective in the devotional meetings. For years after it was published Major Charles Coller's 'I am the resurrection and the life' was featured at the beginning of each Sunday morning meeting.

Brigadier Eva Asplin, who entered the songsters in 1917 as a junior clerk on 'the building' (IHQ) and developed into an outstanding contralto soloist, pays tribute to the influence the members of the brigade had upon her during her eleven years with them. 'I learned so much from them', she testifies, and adds that it was the soulful singing of 'Mine and Thine', Lieut.-Colonel Ernest Rance's setting to Susie Swift's words, that led her to dedicate her life for officership.

The Brigadier has vivid memories of a group of the songsters supporting General Bramwell Booth in the Army's first radio broadcast from the old 2LO studio at Savoy Hill. Captain Leslie Taylor-Hunt sang a 'new song' recently arrived from the USA and not yet published in *The Musical Salvationist*. It was 'The old rugged cross'.

General Bramwell, when the tell-tale red light went off denoting that the broadcast had ended, caused the technicians some consternation by launching into a lengthy prayer on their behalf.

One of the routine duties of the songsters, apart from public commitments, was to rehearse and present manuscript music to the

International Music Board, as their counterpart, the Staff Band, prepared and played new band compositions.

Like so many other Headquarters' sections, the Staff Songsters came to an abrupt end. There had been rumours for some time that their days were numbered. Administrative problems—caused by so many songsters coming from the one department and late returns on Monday mornings from week-end campaigning—these were always the difficulties that prevented the smooth running of such sections.

Perhaps it was no real surprise, therefore, when the songsters were told at a lunch-time practice early in 1928 that the Chief of the Staff had decided the International Headquarters' Songster Brigade would be disbanded. Always master of the situation, Colonel Howard prayed and then calmly announced, 'Comrades, we will sing our last piece together'.

It was the 'Hallelujah!' Chorus, and as no preparations had been made and no organ was available, the redoubtable pioneers sang from memory and without accompaniment—as they had never sung before.

A few weeks before, without knowing it, the songsters had carried out their final campaign at Winton. Sir Dan Godfrey, the renowned conductor of the Bournemouth Symphony Orchestra, presided over the Sunday afternoon programme and had a special words of thanks and congratulations for one of the soloists, Alfred Andrews. His solo was 'Strength Renewed'. A timely motto for the end of an era!

Salvation Singers

It is surprising how many noted Salvation Army songster brigades simply crept into prominence. This certainly goes for the Salvation Singers, who operated from the old Trade Headquarters in Fortress Road, Kentish Town, and then from Salvationist Publishing and Supplies, Ltd., when the new premises were opened at Judd Street, King's Cross, in 1911.

With the success of the Staff Songsters as an impetus, the Secretary for Trade, in the early days of the century, decided that a similar group should be started on his headquarters, confined to officers and employees under his jurisdiction. Colonel Clifford Grinsted was entrusted with the leadership and the Salvation Singers were soon in action.

In 1904 it was thought that official recognition should be given to the singing brigade and a Minute issued by the Chief of the Staff permitted them authentically to exist. The leader was Major (later Colonel) Alfred Braine.

A spirit of healthy rivalry was instantly set up, both the Staff Songsters and Salvation Singers competing for laurels. If they ever shared a platform for a festival, other than at big events, it was never recorded. Each proceeded along its independent path, setting a pattern and building a reputation, until, within weeks of each other, they passed into Army musical history.

It is worth noting that three of the Army's singing pioneers, Carleton, Jackson and Braine, were all soldiers of the Penge Corps at the same time. All were local officers. Each was a forceful personality.

Alfred Braine already had an impressive musical background when he took over the leadership of the Salvation Singers. As the Army's publisher he had the distinction of issuing the first number of The Salvation Army *Band Journal* and the *Tune Book*. After a period as Bandmaster at Croydon Citadel he took over similar duties at Penge, was a member of the International Staff Band and had a number of published songs to his credit.

In 1921 Colonel Braine became the first National Secretary for Bands in the British Territory, and served as Songster Leader at East Finchley.

When the Colonel relinquished the leadership in 1912, Staff-Captain William Starr succeeded him. The Staff-Captain was known as an enthusiastic exponent of the singing art and built upon the firm foundations laid by Clifford Grinsted and Alfred Braine.

At the beginning of the 1st World War two names began to appear on the singers' programmes, the bearers of which were to make their mark in widely different spheres. A brilliant young pianist, Edgar Grinsted, a son of the pioneer leader, was shortly to leave for a distinguished career as a pilot in the newly-formed Royal Flying Corps (later renamed the Royal Air Force) and much later became a Commissioner and Territorial Commander.

The newest addition to the International Music Editorial Department was featured as a concertina soloist. He was Henry Hall, who after war service became an esteemed member of the musical profession and famous as a band leader. His parents remained life-long Salvationists and his sister, Edna, is Mrs Lieut.-Colonel Ernest Barnes, now living in retirement in the London area.

The next leader was Brigadier (later Colonel) Arthur Goldsmith, who was in charge for two years from 1922. Internationally known as a composer of instrumental and vocal music, and as the soprano cornet player in the Staff Band, the Brigadier brought considerable experience to his task and himself wrote many songs and early forms of vocal selections with the Salvation Singers in mind. 'Forward March' and 'Showers of Blessing' are pieces remembered from that period.

In December 1924, after a time of inactivity, the singers were reformed with Staff-Captain (later Lieut.-Colonel) James Valentine as

the Leader, and Adjutant (later Colonel) Charles Cox as the conductor. The organist was Eva Braine, a daughter of the erstwhile
leader, and Eric Ball, who had joined the Music Editorial Department
some three years before, was the pianist. Nellie Garrett continued as
Secretary. An unforgettable character, Nellie had been associated with
the singers for many years and was, in addition, Songster Leader at a
London corps, Newington Green.

Other youthful members were Samuel Hooper and Edith
Goldsmith. These made names for themselves as a vocal soloist and
elocutionist, respectively.

Colonel Cox, as a younger officer, was leader of the Scotland
Territorial Headquarters' Songster Brigade during the short period of
its existence and, upon transferring to London, became a member
of the International Staff Songsters.

With the formation of the Salvationist Publishing and Supplies
Band in 1928, at the express wish of General Bramwell Booth to set a
pattern for smaller bands, it became inevitable that the Salvation
Singers would cease to function. Captain Eric Ball, the Bandmaster,
had led the singers for the final months of their service and with him
and other male members of the Headquarters' staff caught up in the
new section, it was impossible to maintain the vocal group.

There must always be a reluctance to begin mentioning names for
fear of missing some, but any record of the Salvation Singers must
include passing reference to such personalities as Cornwall, Pigott,
Roper and Ibbett, as well as songsters who gave such excellent service
as organist, among them Mrs Colonel Braine, who as Ensign Barnett
had served in this capacity even before her marriage to the Colonel and
continuously afterwards, and Rosina Halsey (Mrs Colonel W. David
Wellman). Mrs Staff-Captain Starr featured as a vocal soloist for the
period of her husband's leadership, and other members who enhanced
the festivals were Brigadier Archie Burgess, with his concertina solos,
and Adjutant Harry Green, an able pianist and happy singer of typical
Army popular songs. The latter, a member of the Canadian Staff
Band, lost his life in the *Empress of Ireland* disaster in 1914.

Judd Street has always been a good music centre. As the home of
musical publications it has attracted Salvationists from all parts of the
world, but in addition to this, many personalities engaged in serving
the needs of musicians have become internationally known. There
have been many attempts to emulate the Salvation Singers by forming
groups of the same kind, but not with any measure of success.

In Judd Street's golden jubilee year (1961) Songster Leader Samuel
Hooper was requested to gather together a singing brigade to do duty
during the celebrations, but this was short-lived.

still in constant use after nearly eighty years. A fourth song from his pen, 'O boundless salvation', will always be known as the Founder's Song.

He sat up all night to write it for the 'Boundless Salvation' campaign held in Great Britain in 1893, and handed the verses to his secretary, Staff-Captain (later Commissioner) Theodore Kitching, upon his arrival at the Founder's home at Hadley Wood at six o'clock the next morning.

The influence of this song is eternal. It was sung at the Royal Albert Hall on 9 May 1912. This was William Booth's last public meeting.

He wrote in his diary: 'The hall was gorged when we arrived. . . . Every seat was occupied and some very inconveniently so. The reception I received when I entered was overwhelming, but alas, when I opened my mouth with the first song, 'O boundless salvation', I found to my astonishment that my voice was broken. The ring of it was wanting and I had to put out the fullest effort possible to fill the building'.

In 1930, responding to a request from Commander Evangeline Booth to write a march to commemorate the golden jubilee of Army work in the United States, John Philip Sousa composed 'The Salvation Army' and included the Founder's Song. When Lieut.-Commissioner William Barrett, then Training Principal in New York, gave the composer the words and music of the song, he was asked to sing a verse so that Sousa might get the Army slant on it. On reaching the refrain:

> The whole world redeeming, so rich and so free,
> Now flowing for all men, come roll over me,

the Commissioner was asked to repeat it. He did so with Sousa joining in with his tenor voice.

The composer studied the words for a few minutes and said: 'Your Founder was a mighty man of God and was certainly inspired when he wrote that hymn. It is a classic and will live on'.

Jane Stoddart, a London journalist, reporting the welcome to General Evangeline Booth as the Army's International Leader in 1934 for *The British Weekly,* said:

> There was a moment at the Royal Albert Hall on Thursday evening when quick ears might have heard a soft rushing, as of ocean waves. Not the Atlantic breakers, for General Booth had come home from her wanderings, and two nations united to honour her, have forgotten the dividing seas. I was thinking of George Fox's version, 'I saw an ocean of life and love flow over the ocean of sin and death'.
>
> Those words may have inspired William Booth's glorious hymn—equal in its opening stanza to any in our language:
>
> > O boundless salvation, deep ocean of love,
> > O fulness of mercy Christ brought from above.

> Ten thousand voices joined in this hymn, to the music of united bands. Great singing, assuredly, while 'rain and wind beat dark December'.

On Founders' Day, 1965, in the midst of the Centenary Celebrations, this great song was included in the service of thanksgiving held in Westminster Abbey. *The Musician* editor, giving an item by item commentary of the proceedings, said: 'Again we hear a flourish of trumpets as the introduction of Major Dean Goffin's arrangement of "O boundless salvation" majestically sounds forth. The Centenary Choir (this definition on the order of service cannot offend the deepest-dyed Salvationist in this setting) joins in singing the Founder's Song. Major Goffin is conducting and the organ adds its weight and approval from time to time.

'It has taken seventy-two years for this song to travel from William Booth's study in his home at Hadley Wood to reach Westminster Abbey, but it has reached here at last—and does not sound out of place'.

Two years later Chalk Farm Band was engaged in one of the memorable European tours that has earned it a record unequalled by any other Army section. Belgium, France and Switzerland had been visited and now the train conveying it from Turin had arrived in Rome. Upon alighting, the International Headquarters' representative travelling with the band was informed by Italy's Officer Commanding, Colonel Jean Bordas, that an invitation had been received for the band to play at the Vatican during its stay in the capital.

This was startling news. Such an ecumenical link-up had not been visualized. The representative felt that the acceptance or not of the summons could not be his responsibility.

A phone call was put through to London to seek the advice of General Frederick Coutts. The General did not give his answer at once, but wanted time to consider the matter and to enlist the opinions of international leaders.

The next morning a call from London gave the information that the visit had been approved by the General, who had two requests to make. He desired that the occasion would be as Army as possible, and that every attempt should be made to sing 'O boundless salvation' in the presence of the Pope.

Two days later, in the Benedictine Chapel of the Vatican, William Booth's song rang out as the Chalk Farm bandsmen, in the presence of 1,500 people, lifted their voices. Pope Paul had left his throne and was descending the steps to greet personally a group of representative people. Four Salvationists were among them.

The original idea was for the band to play suitable hymn tunes as the crowd waited for the arrival of His Holiness. By request of the authorities they played as the Pope was carried into the great chapel and as he left. And what better choice could have been made than the march, 'The invincible Army'?

As the bandsmen formed up to march away, across St Peter's Square, the Vatican Guard sprang to attention to salute them, sightseers pressed forward to take photographs, and a party of English visitors cheered.

A Salvation Army officer who visited Russia in 1958, as a tourist, was interested to hear that the singing of 'O boundless salvation' was a popular feature of Baptist worship in that country and is published in the denominational hymn book.

Mr Bramwell

It is somewhat surprising that William Bramwell Booth, eldest child of William and Catherine, did not have a rank in the Army he helped to organize until he succeeded his father as General in 1912. Even for the thirty-four years he served as Chief of the Staff, he was always referred to as Mr Bramwell.

His first song, 'Living in the fountain', was written on 8 March 1877, the author's twenty-first birthday. Under the title of 'A good soldier's life' it was published in *The Christian Mission Magazine*, February 1878. Another song which first appeared in print that year, and in the same publication, was 'Jesus, Saviour, Thou art mine'.

Two of Bramwell Booth's songs are associated with railway stations. 'Come in, my Lord, come in' was scribbled down on Aldersgate Street Station when he had an hour to wait after passengers, unfriendly toward the Army, prevented his boarding the train home.

The other song, 'O when shall my soul find her rest', was also written on a railway station in the midnight hour as he waited for a train for London.

Emerging from long retirement to speak at a Sunday morning holiness meeting at Clapton Congress Hall in 1951, ninety-year-old Mrs Bramwell Booth recalled the first Army meeting she attended at Whitechapel. 'My spirit was restless', she said. 'That morning the song, "O when shall my soul find her rest", was sung for the first time by Mr Bramwell. He had written the words the night before. The line, "For Thou art almighty to keep", brought light to my soul'.

'My faith looks up to Thee' first appeared in *The Salvationist*, February 1879, and 'I love Thee every hour' in *The War Cry* a year later.

'Oft have I heard Thy tender voice' was written to the tune, 'It was my first cigar, my boys'. Colonel Edward Joy remembered General Bramwell Booth telling him how, one night in his younger days, he paid an organ-grinder a shilling so that he might get hold of the tune correctly. The street musician obliged until the melody was committed to memory.

The authorship of this song was also claimed by Emma Booth-Tucker, Bramwell's sister, and known as the Consul. The writer of her biography, *The Consul*, relates how, when travelling on the Continent, Emma heard the melody sung by an officer, accompanying himself on a guitar. It inspired her to write words to the tune, says the biographer.

Marshal Ballington

In some ways Ballington Booth, it is said, was the most gifted of all the children. He was a combination of the warm sympathy of his mother and the magnetic personality of his father.

Six feet four inches in height, black bearded and strikingly handsome, he was a popular leader. At twenty-two he was in charge of the men's side of officer training.

One writer has said: 'Ballington was beloved by all. On the platform he could play with an audience as a Paderewski can with an instrument. His anecdotes and solos (to an accompaniment on an English concertina) won him a way into the hearts of all.'

Ballington Booth left the Army's ranks in 1896, whilst in charge of the work in the United States, and formed The American Volunteers, of which he became the General. This tragic decision followed a confrontation with his father and brother Bramwell after Ballington had been instructed to farewell after eight years' successful leadership.

He was the composer of many songs, two of which appear in *The Song Book of The Salvation Army*. These are 'The cross that He gave may be heavy' and 'Jesus, Saviour, I am waiting'. Other songs from his pen which became favourites are 'You've carried your burden' and 'Over and over, like a mighty sea', which the USA delegates to the 1894 International Congress introduced into world-wide popular usage.

The Marechale

The eldest daughter and third child of the family became one of the Army's earliest soloists. Her pioneering activities are described elsewhere, but her efforts at song-writing, though few, met with marked success.

'O Lamb of God, Thou wonderful sin-bearer' was written to a French melody and other popular contributions were 'O spotless Lamb of Calvary' and 'When tempted sore to worry', the last named with words set to a popular Swiss tune.

In 1887 the Marechale was married to Arthur Clibborn and together they held several territorial appointments on the Continent of Europe. They resigned their commissions in Janury 1902 due to a disagreement between General William Booth and the Marechale's husband, then Commissioner Booth-Clibborn, on certain points of doctrine and constitution.

The Marechale remained as an earnest evangelical preacher and drew large crowds to her meetings, which she continued to conduct until shortly before her death in 1955.

In May 1934 this gifted leader accepted an invitation to take part in a Thursday holiness meeting at Clapton Congress Hall. She and her husband sang a duet, and the Marechale took for the subject of her address, 'The Violin'. The speaker was introduced by her youngest sister, Commissioner Lucy Booth-Hellberg.

Arthur Booth-Clibborn was also a songwriter, perhaps his best known creation being 'O God of light, O God of love', which is in *The Song Book of The Salvation Army*.

The Consul

Emma Moss Booth was to the women's side of the training home what her brother Ballington was to the men's. She was twenty-two when her father entrusted her with this responsibility and she served in this important appointment for six years, marrying Commissioner Frederick Tucker in 1888.

Her dynamic personality and inspirational leadership earned her the name of Home Mother. Commissioner and Mrs Booth-Tucker (all the Booth daughters retained their family name upon marriage) served in India for some time, but Emma's inability to adjust to the climate made it necessary for them to return.

After a period at International Headquarters they were given command of the United States, upon the secession of Ballington, and the Consul, as she became known, met her death in a railway accident when travelling from Kansas City to Chicago on 29 October 1903. She was forty-three.

Of the Consul's songs the most familiar is 'O my heart is full of music and of gladness', the music of which was written by her husband. It was after he had climbed the stairs of a London omnibus to the upper deck that the melody came to him. Upon arriving home he repeated the tune to her and explained the difficulty of finding suitable words because of the irregular metre.

'You must have special words,' she said, 'something to suit your going up the bus steps'. She there and then wrote the verses of the song, with its ascending chorus, 'O, I'm climbing up the golden stair to Glory'.

The Consul's love for children, her great belief in the possibility of a young life being consecrated to the service of Christ, and her prayerful desire for members of her own family, led to the writing of 'Blessed Jesus, save our children'.

'We the people of Thy host' was composed for officers' councils in New York, for which the first line originally read, 'We the prophets of Thy host'.

Apart from being a composer of music—his melody, 'Tucker', has become forever linked with the Founder's words, 'Thou Christ of burning, cleansing flame'—Commissioner Booth-Tucker was the author of many songs. Of his five in *The Song Book of The Salvation Army*, the best known is undoubtedly 'They bid me choose an easier path' ('I cannot leave the dear old flag'), set to the haunting Scottish melody, 'We'd better bide a wee', thought to have been written at the time Ballington and his wife left the ranks.

The eldest of the Booth-Tuckers' seven children, Mrs Commissioner Motee Sladen, inherited the family's musical gifts and will be remembered for her charming melody, 'Land of pure delight', composed when she was twelve years of age. She also wrote the music of her husband's song, 'Touch me with Thy healing hand, Lord'.

Commandant Herbert

The fifth child and third son of the Founder and Army Mother, Herbert Howard Booth was born to musical stardom. As a learner at the pianoforte keyboard he was the most promising of the children and his beginnings as a songwriter have been recounted in an earlier chapter.

At the age of twenty he was appointed to assist his brother Ballington at the training homes and two years later succeeded him. In those two years (1882-1884) he formed brigades of salvation songsters who toured Britain on a singing-recruiting mission and, with Richard Slater, instituted the Music Department.

Ever alert to pioneering possibilities, he never spared himself from being in the vanguard of all such ventures and still found time to lead the cadets into action. He campaigned extensively in the British Isles and was able to bring into being the poetic and musical inspirations which were queuing up in his mind waiting to be born. It is not surprising that, in 1888, he broke down in health.

His devoted and loving father, fully realizing Herbert's value to the Army, relieved him of all responsibilities and sent him on a world-wide tour, to visit countries where the Movement was established, encourage the forces and report back to the General.

When s.s. *Doric,* which sailed from London's Royal Albert Docks in October 1888, made its first stop in Plymouth Harbour, anchor was cast for the reception and dispatch of mail before the rigours of the Atlantic were faced. Among the many communications received by Herbert was one from his father, who wrote: 'My dear boy, I cannot tell you how much I love you, how much I expect from you, how much I live again in you. No man living—at least, not many men—have the mighty possibilities of usefulness that God has given to you, my dear Herbert, and I rely on your rising up to meet them. . . .'

On his return to London, Herbert became Commandant for Britain, an appointment comparable to that of today's British Commissioner. Still he worked without let-up, his many interests including the establishment of mammoth spectacular events with music at their centre.

Territorial leadership in Canada and Australasia followed and it was from the latter command that the Commandant, with his wife, resigned his officership. Pressed by newspaper men for an explanation, Herbert refused to comment other than to say that the reasons were 'personal and conscientious'.

Herbert attended his father's funeral at Abney Park in 1912, saluting as the old warrior's coffin was lowered into the grave and immediately turning to greet his brother, the new General, with a kiss. There was much of the soldier in the Commandant. One wonders what his thoughts were that day as band after band, in the long march along the Embankment, passed International Headquarters and on through the stilled city streets playing his funeral march, 'Promoted to Glory', which he had composed at the time of his mother's passing.

'As a songwriter', said Richard Slater, 'Herbert Booth claims first place among the poets and composers of the Army, not only because of the great number of his songs, but likewise because of the great and varied merits of his work for Army purposes and the number of his songs in constant use as congregational songs and choruses.'

Recent historians have questioned the authenticity of Herbert Booth's songwriting. It has been suggested that Richard Slater could have been the author or composer of many songs bearing the Commandant's name. This theory has no real basis and is hard to accept.

Herbert Booth's songs bear the hallmark of genius, both in the nature of the sentiment expressed and the manner of expression. His music, too, has a quality that assures it a place among the finest melody and harmony published by the Army or any other organization.

It has to be said that Herbert Booth worked under considerable pressure, his main duties having no direct connection with poetry and music. We have this on the word of Slater himself, whose integrity is beyond question and who would not go out of his way to eulogize Herbert's songwriting if he himself were the rightful author.

In the nature of his responsibilities as Head of the Music Department, Slater would make himself available when the Commandant wished him to take down a new song that had come to him. As an able organist, Herbert would play the melody and harmony as he had conceived it, adding the words as he played. Slater's task was to transfer these thoughts to manuscript paper and later to edit and embellish, with the approval of the composer.

The credit therefore belongs to Herbert Booth and none can deny him the honour of being the author and composer of such masterpieces as 'While He's waiting', 'Grace there is my every debt to pay', 'To the front the cry is ringing', 'I will not doubt the heart that loved me', 'Let me love Thee', 'Promoted to Glory' and scores of others. Among his sets of words only are also masterpieces: 'Lord, through the Blood of the Lamb that was slain', 'From every stain made clean', 'Joy, freedom, peace' and 'Let me hear Thy voice'.

Is it to underestimate Slater to suggest that his own songs did not retain the consistent quality with which Herbert Booth's songs are marked? Would the Father of Salvation Army music have given his old chief so much credit if he thought otherwise?

'Promoted to Glory' is said to be one of the finest funeral marches ever written, and that includes the classics of Handel and Chopin.

In September 1890 Herbert Booth was married to Cornelie Schoch, one of the three talented daughters of a Dutch military colonel who, on becoming a Salvationist, was given the same rank in The Salvation Army. She is the writer of 'Bring to the Saviour thy burden of grief', 'A perfect trust' and 'Holy Spirit, seal me I pray'. At the time of their wedding Commandant and Mrs Booth issued *Songs of Peace and War*, an impressive collection of their own songs.

Commander Eva

William Booth always referred to his fourth daughter, Evangeline Cory, as his 'little Christmas box' because she was born on December 25, in the year of the Army's birth, 1865.

As Herbert was appointed at a tender age to assist Ballington in the training of cadets, so Eva, at nineteen, joined her sister Emma in the leadership of future women officers. Two years later she was given charge of the thriving West End centre of Great Western Hall (later Marylebone Corps) and also served as Field Commissioner before being appointed as Territorial Commander for Canada.

Upon the death of her sister Emma she was transferred to the United States where she served as National Commander for thirty years, until her election as the Army's fourth General in 1934.

Portraits of Evangeline Booth seen strumming on her harp or sitting at a portable organ are legion. They reveal the actress in her, but there is no doubt that her greatest relaxation at the end of a busy and problem-packed day was to play gently until a song was born.

'Dark shadows were falling', with the moving chorus, 'The wounds of Christ are open', 'Bowed beneath a garden shade', 'And yet He will Thy sins forgive', 'I bring Thee all' and 'Star in the East' are among her best words and loveliest of melodies. These and others were incorporated in *Songs of the Evangel*, published in 1928, an enlarged edition appearing ten years later.

'The world for God' was written in 1934 in the few weeks between her farewell from her forces in the USA and her welcome in London as General. Her first task upon assuming office was to call Salvationists to an all-out offensive against sin and darkness under the campaign title of 'The world for God'.

The song was sung for the first time by a chorus of nearly 1,000 songsters at her welcome meeting in the Royal Albert Hall on 6 December 1934.

'The words and the music stirred the hearts of Salvationists to their very depths', reported *The Bandsman and Songster*. The song was a clarion call to a fresh and mighty endeavour. Then the grand volume of sound was hushed as the lone voice of Major Herbert Barker, clear as crystal, rang out the General's first command, '*I call to arms the soldiers of the Blood and Fire*'.

Like her brother Herbert, Evangeline needed a capable amanuensis to commit her inspirations to paper. Brigadier William Broughton, Erik Leidzén, Commissioner Gösta Blomberg and Eric Ball gave help in this way, a service the General appreciated. The two of these still living vividly remember the experiences.

Commissioner Blomberg, who joined her staff as a secretary after the death of Lieut.-Commissioner Richard Griffith, witnessed the springing forth from the General's mind of many of her songs, her hands on the keys of her favourite Sankey organ.

'Many a morning when I put in appearance at the General's home at Esher', says the Commissioner, 'she met me with the words, "I had such a wonderful tune in the night but I am afraid it has gone". By and by, when the General was sitting at the organ, fragments of the tune came back and I had the privilege of writing down the new melody'.

The Major, as he then was, then played the melody through at the General's request, while she sat listening. Her conception of correct 'classical' harmony sometimes clashed with the 'modernistic' harmonies provided by her secretary.

'Your suggestions, Major', she would say, 'may be very beautiful and correct, but our people won't sing these songs if you dress them up in too elaborate a dress.'

Soon after her arrival in London to take up world leadership, the General sought the help of Captain Eric Ball in preparing the final edition of her *Songs of the Evangel*. This was never an official assignment, the young officer needing to be 'spirited away' from his Judd Street office in order to meet the General. After forty years Eric admits that his long and frequent absences were difficult to explain to his superiors!

'The General graciously requested the use of the caretaker's small apartment at the top of the I.H.Q. building', Eric remembers. 'There, hidden away, we sat together at the piano. I played her songs and we would discuss them, criticizing, amending. She would accept criticism readily, but knew what she wanted.

' "You don't like that chord, do you, Ball?" '

' "No, General, I don't".

'Smiling, her hand upon my arm, she said: "But I want you to like it" '.

Experts may consider General Eva to have been a better poet than a composer—this may have stemmed from her gifts as an orator—but there is a whimsical charm about her music that makes it an ideal, unobtrusive vehicle for conveying to the heart the intrinsic message of the words.

Commissioner Lucy

In childhood and early womanhood, Lucy Milward Booth, the youngest of the family, suffered indifferent health and found great comfort for her sensitive spirit in giving expression to her love for music, and the desire to create new melodies as well as verses.

Her first serious effort at songwriting was 'Keep on believing', for which she also composed the music. For some years the words were accredited to Commissioner Mildred Duff. Lucy's explanation is important:

'This was the first of many songs I composed. I was, I think, about seventeen or eighteen years of age, and sick at the time, my chest causing my darling mother some anxiety. The doctor had called at our old home, "Rookwood", and whilst my mother was speaking to him, I went to the piano and played the tune.

'Later Commissioner Duff helped me with the rhyming of the words, but the thought contained in them was quite my own, and springs from the incident I mentioned'. Soon after the song was composed, the words hung on the walls of nearly every slum officers' quarters in London.

Lieut.-Colonel Slater sought to encourage the composer by providing words to her melodies. These include 'For me has the Saviour died', 'Fighting for the King' and 'Filled is my heart with grateful praise'.

Two of the Commissioner's best-known songs are 'Sins of years are all numbered', written in a crowded railway carriage of an early morning train from Clacton-on-Sea to London after visiting her dying mother, and 'Be Thou my guiding star', penned whilst prostrate with grief following a broken romance.

Commissioner Lucy was married in 1894 to Colonel Emmanuel Hellberg, a gifted Swedish officer stationed at International Headquarters. Following the wedding, conducted by the Chief of the Staff in the absence of the General, they sailed for service in India, where the wife became the Territorial Commander and the husband her Chief Secretary. Ceylon (now Sri Lanka) was included in the command.

After serving with his wife in charge of Switzerland and France, Commissioner Booth-Hellberg was promoted to Glory in 1909, after which his widow continued as a Territorial Commander in Denmark, South America and Norway. She was promoted to Glory from Sweden in 1953.

In paying tribute to a remarkable family of music-makers, space must be found for a mention of Catherine, the mother, whose patience, love and loyalty, often in the face of great suffering cemented that family together and who toiled incessantly for its happiness. At her funeral service in London's Olympia, Herbert's 'Promoted to Glory' was used for the first time. At the funeral service in Abney Park his song, 'Blessed Lord, in Thee is refuge', was sung as the coffin was lowered into the grave.

After the committal, as William Booth and his family (except Ballington who was in America) stepped down from the specially erected platform, 10,000 voices (tickets had restricted admission to this number) took up the strains of 'To the front the cry is ringing'

('Victory for me'), also written and composed by the Army Mother's youngest son.

Catherine Booth, who confessed to not knowing a note of music, was the gentle power behind the throne, living long enough to see her gifted sons and daughters become international leaders in the Army she and William founded, and being spared the heartache of later schisms which brought so much sorrow to her beloved William.

CHAPTER FIFTEEN

CREATING THE SONGS

THE first 'poet laureate' of The Salvation Army was Colonel William Pearson. Born in Derby in 1832, he became an evangelist in The Christian Mission in 1874 and gave William Booth steadfast support in the leaders' meetings which caused so much dissension in those formative years.

In 1878, at the time of the change of name, he wrote 'Come, join our Army, to battle we go', which was published in *The Salvationist,* February 1879, under the title, 'Song of The Salvation Army'. The song was inspired by the sound of the chimes of Bradford Town Hall playing 'Ring the bell, watchman', to which melody it was written.

There is not sufficient available space to refer to all twenty-three of Pearson's songs which appear in *The Song Book of The Salvation Army*. Two will represent the others. 'O Thou God of every nation' was written for the opening of the Clapton Congress Hall in May 1882. Of this song Lieut.-Colonel Richard Slater said: 'It comes nearest of all others to supplying the Army with a song of a national anthem type. . . . It is truly Army in terms, language and sentiments'.

'Jesus, give Thy Blood-washed Army' was written for the first International Congress in 1886. A verse omitted from the present song book seems to have significance:

> Cover land and sea with soldiers,
> Hell's dark legions backward hurl;
> Make the Army stronger, bolder,
> More triumphant flags unfurl;
> . With salvation
> Make us conquerors of the world.

Pearson also wrote 'Joy, joy, joy, there is joy in The Salvation Army', from which the title of this book is taken, as was that of its companion, *Play the music, play!*

The influence of the Fry family on Salvation Army music has already been described. Charles Fry, the father and first bandmaster, was already a songwriter before he became a Salvationist. As 'Ye sons of God, awake to glory', set to 'The Marseillaise', was published in *The Christian Mission Hymn Book* before 1878, it is thought that this was written prior to his linking-up with Salvationists at Salisbury. He is the author of a number of songs, most of them set to secular melodies.

Frederick William Fry, the Army's first bandsman and eldest son of Charles, blossomed as a writer of words and composer of music in the adventurous 1880s. 'My sins are under the Blood', 'I'll stand for Christ' and 'To Thy Cross I come, Lord' are from his pen.

Colonel Fred Hawkes, Head of the International Music Editorial Department from 1913 to 1936, regarded his predecessor in that appointment, Lieut.-Colonel Richard Slater, as the Army's 'Songwriter Number One', and this could well be true, despite the attempts of Slater to confer this title upon others. His record may not be overtaken for some years, if at all.

Of Slater's published songs he wrote the words of 127, the music of 166 and the words and music of 294. Another 264 were in manuscript at the time of his passing in 1939, making a grand and impressive total of 851.

The story of Slater's conversion and of his pioneer work in the Music Department, set up by Herbert Booth, is well known. Much of his time was taken up in shaping up the efforts of novice writers, to prepare their humble creations for publication, if he thought there was merit in them. But the Army must for ever be grateful that he made time to let the streams of inspiration flow from his own heart and mind.

'Jesus, see me at Thy feet', 'God is near Thee', 'I think of all His sorrow' and 'Ever Thine', the last named written on the first anniversary of his conversion, will live as long as the Army itself, as will 'At peace with God', sung at the composer's funeral in a quiet Margate cemetery.

Slater made no attempt to be profound. He wrote for the times and the people of the times, as his leaders asked him to do. The beauty of that simplicity lives on.

Other early-day writers were Harry Davis, a packing-case maker who was one of the first soldiers of Whitechapel Corps; J. D. Allan, who was private secretary to Herbert Booth before resigning for health reasons and becoming a Congregational minister; James Bateman (to be referred to later); Thomas C. Marshall, converted at Regent Hall and later serving as an Army journalist in the USA; Harry Hill and George Scott Railton. Hill, with Slater and Fred Fry, constituted the first staff of the music department.

Mark Sanders was a writer whose gifts were encouraged and nurtured by Richard Slater. A son of poor parents, he became blind when three years old. His love for music was apparent whilst at school and he developed into a skilful player on various instruments as well as becoming an acceptable singer.

In 1882, after meeting the Army and becoming converted the

previous year, 'Blind Mark', as from then on he was affectionately known, became a special campaigner, working first in Devon and Cornwall. Five years later he assisted in pioneering Army work in the West Indies.

The latter part of his life was spent at Salt Lake City, USA, where he remained a Salvationist until his promotion to Glory in 1943. His gravestone bears the inscription: 'Singer-composer, Pioneer missionary. Lovingly remembered by West Indian Salvationists.'

The name of Charles Coller first became known when he was a young bandsman at Regent Hall. Service with the Household Troops Band, and then the International Staff Band, added to his reputation. His first song was published in April 1895. There is a touch of thoroughness about his songs, which include 'Salvation! Shout salvation', sung by the congregation at the Centenary Service of Thanksgiving in Westminster Abbey in 1965.

Another prolific songwriter whose verses, choruses and melodies are sung every Sunday in some part of the Army world is Sidney E. Cox. Beginning in 1915 with 'You can tell out the sweet story', this Northampton-born evangelist continued to write popular songs to the end of his life. 'I was wandering in the wilderness', 'The Saviour sought and found me', 'I am amazed that a Saviour should die' and 'God's love is wonderful' are but a few.

He served as an officer for thirty-five years—in Canada and then the United States—and resigned in 1944 to devote his time to other evangelical work.

From his earliest days as a bandsman at Folkestone, Colonel Edward Joy was a songwriter, and remained so until his promotion to Glory in 1949. His first song, published in April 1894, was 'The March to Victory'. With the passing of the years his inventive power developed, and some of his most effective compositions appeared in later editions of *The Musical Salvationist*.

Some of the author's love of fun and good humour, expressed so noticeably in his book, *The Old Corps*, is reflected in such songs as 'It's a fair "dinkum" Army', 'Cheer up, comrades' and 'Come along to Beulah'. But he will be remembered mainly for his deeply devotional contributions: 'All my days and all my hours', 'All your anxiety', 'O that in me the mind of Christ' and the verses of 'Jesus, Thou art everything to me'. He served as Editor-in-Chief for the Canada West Territory and finally as Editor of the South African *War Cry*.

Brigadier Ruth Tracy wrote her first 'jingle' when she was a small schoolgirl, about an elder brother's love affairs, fact and fiction interwoven. Later, when she obtained employment in the Appointments Department at the Home Office of International

Headquarters, then at 149 Queen Victoria Street, near to Blackfriars Station, her boss, Staff-Captain (later Commissioner) James Hay, saw one of her merry poems, a take-off about departmental happenings, and called her into his office. Expecting a reprimand, she was relieved to hear an earnest suggestion that the gift should be put to better purpose and used for the Kingdom of God.

'How?' she asked, bewildered.

'Write a song for *The War Cry*', he said.

In those days the back page of the Army's official organ was devoted each week to original songs. Many future noted songwriters had their first humble efforts published in this way. Ruth took the Staff-Captain's advice as a sort of command, and never looked back.

Brigadier Tracy spent the whole of her officership at International Headquarters, mostly in the Editorial Department, and was greatly in demand as a provider of songs for special occasions. Bramwell Booth, Thomas Coombs and James Hay were among those to make such requests, from which sprang forth such Army classics as 'I've a Friend of friends the fairest', 'Send out Thy light and Thy truth, Lord', 'Where are now the doubts that hindered', 'Lord, I come to Thee, beseeching' and 'Lord, I pray that I may know Thee'.

Australia is proud of its own outstanding songwriter, Colonel Arthur Arnott. As a young man of twenty-three he listened to an Army open-air meeting in St Leonard's Park, North Sydney, attended the indoor meeting, knelt at the Mercy Seat when the invitation was given, and commenced fifty years' service for his Master.

For forty years he conducted the annual young people's demonstration held during the congress at Melbourne, and it was for this event that many of his most popular songs were composed, among them 'I'd rather be a little thing climbing up', 'The birds upon the tree-tops' and 'Some day I'll see His blessed face'.

With Colonel Joy he shared the authorship of 'Jesus, Thou art everything to me', supplying the words of the chorus. This song was written to a melody which Colonel Arnott had heard at a Sunday-school anniversary and was not able to trace. He claims to have altered the music to avoid possible copyright problems.

This author's 'Home is home, however lowly' owes its being to a request made by a home league local officer in Melbourne for a song suitable in a demonstration, and 'Tell them in the east and in the west' was composed on board ship as Australian delegates were returning from the 1914 International Congress.

The Colonel was promoted to Glory in 1942. Fifteen years later Sir William Angliss, well known as Australia's meat 'king', in his will left £10,000 for the erection of a memorial to Colonel Arnott. This

Salvationist songwriter has another claim to fame. The family of biscuit makers from which he came 'dedicated' a product in his memory. This is known as the 'SAO' biscuit, the initials standing for 'Salvation Army officer'.

Among Canada's many songwriters were Professor Wiggins, who is best remembered for 'Swing those gates ajar', and Envoy William Hawley. The Envoy was born at Belleville, Ontario, from which corps General Arnold Brown became an officer. It is not without significant humour that Hawley's first song, written in 1898, should have been 'From the General down to me'.

William Hawley's best-known song is 'A light came out of darkness', with the challenging chorus, 'Shall you? Shall I?' He died in 1929 in Calgary, Alberta.

Another early-day songwriter who ended his days in Alberta was Gustavus Grozinsky. He was promoted to Glory from an Army eventide home in Edmonton in 1937.

Grozinsky is perhaps unique in Army history. He was born in Moscow. His father, in the days of Czarist Russia, became a marked man because of his political views. Eventually he was arrested and sentenced to death, a punishment that was later commuted to life banishment in Siberia.

Some time later he managed to escape, to communicate with his wife and two children and settle with them in Cronstadt. After a time the family moved to England and lived near the Walworth Road, in South London. Gustavus, attracted by the music of an Army open-air meeting, knelt at the Mercy Seat at Camberwell.

Becoming an officer, his first appointment was to the far north of Scotland, where his Captain had oversight of the 'Island Section', which included Wick and Thurso on the mainland and the Orkneys and Shetlands. During the severe winter the Captain and Lieutenant were 'snowed in' for some days, with no outside communication and little food and fuel.

The Lieutenant decided to go to bed to keep warm and to save food. Downstairs, the Captain, depressed and discouraged, wrote out his resignation. Suddenly the Lieutenant appeared in the doorway and, to the accompaniment of his stringed instrument, began to sing his latest song, 'I'll be true! I'll be true!'

The Captain destroyed the letter and remained true to his calling until, as Lieut.-Colonel William Starling, he was promoted to Glory in 1952.

When General Albert Orsborn came to his high office in 1946 he was already acknowledged as one of the Army's most outstanding songwriters. His first song was published in *The Musical Salvationist* forty years before, the music having been composed by his fellow cadet and sergeant, Harry Howard, who as a Captain was promoted to Glory at twenty-three years of age whilst serving in India.

Albert Orsborn inherited an instinct for the rhythm and music in poetry from his father, but he dared not show his early inspirations to his sterner parent. Encouragement came from his mother and later from Commissioner Frederick Booth-Tucker, under whose direction the future General worked as a junior clerk in the 'Foreign Office' of those days. The Commissioner taught him the fundamentals of poetry writing.

It was Commissioner T. Henry Howard who set the poet's feet in the right direction, for he was then more interested in the light and satirical.

'Orsborn', he said, 'will you promise me that anything you write shall in future bear the addendum: "Written to the glory of God and for practical purposes only"?'

During his eight years of international leadership song inspiration continued to flow. 'I know Thee who Thou art', 'Shepherd, hear my prayer' and 'Though the waves and billows are gone o'er me' are worthy successors to 'The Old Wells', 'From a hill I know' and 'Crowned with thorns', meriting inclusion in *The Song Book of The Salvation Army* with fifteen others from his gifted pen.

It must not be overlooked that General Orsborn also wrote music. His name has appeared in *The Musical Salvationist*, showing he supplied the melodies for 'They are gone on a journey', 'Tell the truth to Jesus' and 'I know Thee who Thou art' ('Brantwood').

A selection of the General's best-loved songs has been published in book form under the title of *The Beauty of Jesus*. His aptitude for writing words to popular secular melodies will be discussed later.

If it is true, as is claimed, that The Salvation Army has produced few real poets, then Will J. Brand was unquestionably one of the few.

For years this sensitive, ascetic Salvationist wrote poetry for the sheer enjoyment of it, as well as to express much of the deep feeling of his soul. He was launched on his belated but prolific songwriting career after two Thornton Heath songsters billeted at his home during a specialing campaign. One of them was Mrs Alfred Vickery, wife of the Thornton Heath songster leader and sister of Brigadier (later Commissioner) Alfred Gilliard, Editor of *The War Cry*.

She was shown some of Will's verses and immediately advised him to send them to her brother. Sensing the creative value of this 'new discovery', the editor passed them to Colonel Bramwell Coles, then Head of the International Music Editorial Department. That link-up started a close friendship between the poet and musician which resulted in Brother Brand becoming the Army's most prolific verse-writer for thirty years from the mid-1930s.

Fourteen of his songs appear in *The Song Book of The Salvation Army*, the majority of these originally set to music written by leading Salvationist composers. Will Brand learned the art of placing himself in the way of inspiration, which meant that he found no difficulty in producing the right kind of song for the right occasion when asked to do so—which was frequently.

'When from sin's dark hold Thy love had won me', 'Set forth within the sacred word' and 'Earthly kingdoms rise and fall' are among his songs that came into being 'by special request'. While it must be recognized that this poet and verse-maker provided a number of melodies for his own words, it is equally true that his most successful songs are those set to music by other composers.

Not long before Will Brand's promotion to Glory in 1977, General Clarence Wiseman, at a weekly prayer meeting at International Headquarters, presented the poet with a collection of his own works, published under the title of *With Sword and Song*, and just off the press. In this way Salvationists at the Army's heart honoured the veteran who, nearly seventy years before, had commenced work at the old '101' as a junior in the stationery department.

A consistent songwriter for many years is Lieut.-Colonel Doris Rendell. This interest came about through severe illness, and since that time this charming personality, who left a Government department in Whitehall to become an officer, has produced set after set of verses and choruses. Many leading composers of today pay tribute to her interest and encouragement, not only with a written note or telephone call, but often by passing on verses to make sure that the promising writer 'keeps at it'.

Some of her songs are in the song book, but her main contribution to Army service has been the many works to her credit published in *The Musical Salvationist*.

From the earliest days of the Movement literary ability and songwriting prowess seem to have gone hand in hand. Facility with words would appear naturally to lead to an instinct for writing verse. Countless Army journalists and authors have progressed along this way.

One of them is Lieut.-Commissioner Arch R. Wiggins, who, like Lieut.-Colonel Rendell, will be remembered for many *Musical Salvationist* gems. Collaboration with some of the best composers has assured the Commissioner of a place in Army history, and 'The greatest of these', 'If on my soul a trace of sin remaineth', 'Show us Thy glory' and 'Thou art the way' will live on, as will 'The old drummer', 'The Great Call' and 'Zachary More', although cast in a different mould.

The Commissioner was Editor of *The Musician* for thirteen years, a record period, and also served as Editor-in-Chief in Australia before returning to London as Editor of the *International War Cry*, later being appointed Editor-in-Chief.

Salvationists are indebted to Lieut.-Commissioner Wiggins for his life of Richard Slater, *The Father of Salvation Army Music,* written during the years of the 2nd World War, and for volumes four and five of *The History of The Salvation Army.* 'A.R.W.' was one of the Army's most versatile personalities and excelled as a preacher, raconteur and elocutionist. His 'one man shows', in which he took all parts of the dialogue in turn, were ahead of their time.

Colonel Catherine Baird is another 'editorial and literary' whose songs and poems have adorned the Army's treasury of print. After serving as an officer in South Africa and the USA Central Territory, the Colonel was appointed to International Headquarters as Editor of *The Young Soldier* in 1934, thus beginning an association of nearly thirty years, when she retired from active service with the appointment of Literary Secretary.

The vision of the mystic that she is comes through clearly in her poetic writings, and the high standard she sets is shown in all of them. 'O Love, revealed on earth in Christ', 'We're in God's Army and we fight' and 'When Jesus looked o'er Galilee', perhaps her best-known songs, contain the essence of sound doctrine, deep spiritual insight and religious faith.

Other outstanding songwriters with an editorial or literary background include Colonel Mrs Ivy Mawby and Lieut.-Colonel Miriam Richards. Both are among the large number who so willingly permit inspiration to flow so that the demands of composers might be met.

Although neither has contributed to the present song book, each has a formidable list of successes to her name. 'In the love of Jesus' (Ivy Mawby) and 'Just where He needs me' (Miriam Richards) will not easily be erased from the mind. Miriam Richards is also the writer of many songs for children, some of which appear in *The Young People's Song Book of The Salvation Army.*

CHAPTER SIXTEEN

DEVELOPING THE MUSIC

FROM the earliest days of songster brigade history musical stars have from time to time risen on the horizon desirous of meeting the particular need of such sections and, in many cases, preparing for the future. At first vocal compositions were required to be simple, but effective, and plenty of material was available for this purpose.

Then came the progressive music composers. The increasing interest in group singing and the natural desire to secure more challenging pieces encouraged more difficult compositions. Every generation of Salvationists has thrown up its progressives in this realm and this ever-recurring phenomenon has been acknowledged with gratitude.

Much credit for this is due to the foundations laid by Lieut.-Colonel Richard Slater, first Head of the International Music Editorial Department, and his successor, Colonel Fred Hawkes. Colonel Hawkes is regarded as the architect of Army music, always pressing forward with new ideas and not wilting under the constant rebuffs and misgivings.

The attempt to break out of the shackles of the verse and chorus type of composition began to come in the years following the end of the 1st World War. Oliver Cooke was one of the foremost. He will be remembered for 'I know a fount', but he also wrote such 'revolutionary' numbers as the swinging 'The Lord's Brigade' and one or two scriptural arrangements which became firm favourites with the International Staff Songsters and Salvation Singers.

Early in the 1920s Colonel Hawkes composed 'Bless the Lord, O my soul' and Bandmaster George Marshall 'The Lord is my Shepherd', both settings of adjacent psalms. These pieces were distinctly before their time. Not many brigades could do justice to them, but it was a step in the right direction and set a pattern for future song composers.

Colonel Arthur Goldsmith was another who catered for the needs of the ever-improving vocal sections. His stirring and demanding 'Forward March' became immediately popular, as did 'Seek ye the Lord' and 'Showers of Blessing'. His solo, 'When the sky is blue above you', quickly found its way into the soloist's repertoire.

The words of this were written by Mrs Annie Lynn. After being dismissed by her employers in Scotland for becoming a Salvationist,

she was given work as manageress of the Dressmaking Department of
the old Trade Headquarters in Glasgow. A member of the staff was
Ensign (later Colonel) Goldsmith, who encouraged her to write verses.

The Colonel not only set music to her words himself, but introduced her to other composers. This led to a long list of published
compositions, Lieut.-Colonel Klaus Ostby, the Slater of Scandinavia,
and Bandmaster Marshall being among those who provided music to
her words.

So prolific was Arthur Goldsmith as a composer that, to avoid the
impression he was 'hogging' the scene, he began using pseudonyms.
These included J. H. Gray, J. Hargraves, Legrand, E. Sargent and
G. Ambrose. The composer's initials, A.R.G., can be seen clearly in
each of them.

Toward the end of the 1920s quite advanced vocal music began to
arrive from the United States. The composer was Erik Leidzén, and he
had the added advantage of being able to provide his own words. 'Do
your best!', 'We're sure of victory' (with its intriguing spoken
'Where?') and 'Lay Thy load of sorrow' were promptly taken up by
the Assurance Songsters and soon brigades in all parts of Britain were
'having a go'. With independent accompaniments being issued for
the first time, pianists were put on their mettle to meet the challenge
of the new age.

Another name coming to the fore, also from the USA, was that of
Staff-Captain Kristian Fristrup, with bright melodic lines and happily-
phrased lines which he wrote himself. 'Nicely saved!' enhanced many
programmes in that era.

The next decade witnessed the greatest advance in songster
efficiency. Capable leaders were being persuaded to take over,
whereas up till then the songster brigade was regarded as the
'Cinderella' of the corps. Later there was a temporary setback when
many songster leaders, successful in that role, were commissioned as
bandmasters.

Songster selections came into their own in the 1930s. Foremost in
the field was Lieut.-Colonel Ernest Rance. Several verse and chorus
settings from his pen had appeared earlier, ever since he was a young
Lieutenant, but the international competitions of 1933-4 inspired
such numbers as 'Song of songs', 'Our glorious heritage' (words by
Doris Rendell) and 'Melody-Makers'. In the main he wrote his own
words in those days.

Having shone the torch upon a potential golden age of vocal
composition, the Colonel latterly concentrated upon the creating of
lovely melodies which enhanced such established words as 'Would you
know why I love Jesus?' ('The Reason'), 'Pass me not, O loving

Saviour' ('My humble cry') and 'When there's love at home'. He also supplied memorable music to General Orsborn's 'Shepherd, hear my prayer', and numerous settings to words written by distinguished Army poets.

In his own brand of song-making Ernest Rance has few equals, if any. His expertise on the concertina gives him a rare conception of width of harmony, and this experience has revealed itself in all his songs, with telling results.

This period saw the development of the extended sessional song. General Orsborn, in 1932, was Chief Side Officer for Men at the International Training College. The 'Torchbearers' session was in residence and the Colonel, as he then was, wrote the sessional song. Captain Eric Ball provided the stirring music. The pattern was set. 'Witnesses' and 'The Awakeners' followed, by the same writer and composer, and then with Colonel Orsborn's transfer to New Zealand, the composer continued the good work aided by a variety of collaborators.

Songsters were deeply gratified when it was seen that Eric Ball was bringing to his vocal compositions the skill and feeling that had already marked his band works. In the early days of the 2nd World War, 'A prayer for courage' (for which he also wrote the words) and a women's voice composition, 'In the secret of Thy presence' (Albert Orsborn's words) were published, but the emergency and depletion of sections meant that both masterpieces were lost for more than twenty years.

Eric himself deserves thanks for these revivals. The first song became the basic theme of his tone poem, 'Song of Courage', and the second was incorporated in his meditation, 'Sanctuary'. Songster leaders quickly introduced the 'new' melodies to their brigades.

It took an understandably long time for songster brigades to get into their stride at the end of the 2nd World War. Thanks to a few enthusiastic leaders who were anxious to pick up the threads, the renaissance came and the composers provided the wherewithal of the continuing march forward.

Colonel Fred Grant, for so long the proficient organist for the Assurance Songsters, wrote a number of bright, scintillating through-settings and special arrangements, including 'The King's Highway', 'The Lord's Brigade' and 'This is the day that the Lord has made' (words by Brigadier Lilian Mullins). His soprano solo, 'Lord of every perfect gift' (words by Doris Rendell), had already been featured extensively by the best vocalists before the war, and his contributions to *The Musical Salvationist,* if sporadic, were always welcomed.

The songs of Colonel Charles Skinner, later Head of the Musical

Editorial Department, began to appear at frequent intervals. Ten years before he had made his début with 'I love the Lord', and the 'Intercessors' sessional song was followed by a long line of songs, all carefully constructed and ably clothed in appealing harmony—and always conveying a message to the listeners.

'Is it nothing to you?' (words by Albert Mingay), 'On the threshold' (words by Walter Windybank) and 'Likeness to Christ' (words by H. Benjamin Blackwell) fall into this category, and the Colonel's arrangements of 'I heard the voice of Jesus say' ('Belmont') and 'Praise the Lord, the Almighty' ('Lobe den Herren') are still utilized. 'St Teresa', from his pen, has an honoured place in the Army's tune book.

Mrs Skinner is also a composer, the tune 'Armadale' being the best known. Her mother, Mrs Elizabeth Cossar, wrote the melody bearing her surname, being set, in 1912, to the words, 'My Jesus, I love Thee'. This music also is in the tune book.

Another composer who helped to develop the vocal selection was Songster Leader Stanley Piper. 'March of the soldier', 'The coming of the Light' and 'Climbing up the golden stair' are settings from his pen and there are many others.

The exquisite harmonies of Bandmaster George Marshall have always appealed to songsters. 'The greatest of these' has already been referred to, and others of a devotional character are, 'In the stillness' (words by Reginald Woods), 'Be with us when we pray' (words by Reginald Woods) and 'Grant us Thy peace' (words by Ivy Mawby).

'A song was born' is unique among the bandmaster's vocal compositions. In 1929 George Marshall sent Staff-Captain (later Lieut.-Commissioner) Arch Wiggins a musical setting in four-part harmony in the hope that he would supply the words. Although the music made a tremendous impact upon the Staff-Captain, he could not find inspiration to write suitable words.

Some twenty-seven years later, learning of the passing of his friend and comrade, he took the music from his file and showed it to Colonel Albert Jakeway, Head of the Music Editorial Department. The Colonel expressed surprise that so excellent a composition had not seen the light of day earlier.

A few days later Lieut.-Commissioner Wiggins attended George Marshall's funeral and took the music with him. On the return train journey from South Shields to London he wrote 'A song was born'. George Marshall had unknowingly written his 'requiem' more than a quarter of a century before.

The song tells the bandmaster's story within the compass of twenty-nine lines. It was one of the Commissioner's regrets that so many songster leaders did not explain this fact before their brigades sang the song.

Members of the Music Editorial Department throughout the years have added their quota to the amassing of vocal compositions. Colonel Bramwell Coles, some years after his first march was published, launched out into the songwriting field with 'Sound forth the praises', for which he provided words and music. As the needs presented themselves, so did the music editor seek to meet that need. In collaboration with such poets as Commissioner Alfred Gilliard, Lieut.-Commissioner Wiggins and Will Brand, he provided serviceable music which fulfilled its function of conviction and conversion.

'Here at the Cross in this sacred hour', for which he also wrote the words, has earned an established place in Army hymnology. 'Why hang your harp on the willow?' (words by Harry French) reveals his whimsical sense of humour, and the tune, 'Coles', set to 'Rock of ages cleft for me', remains as a monument to his incomparable record of Army music-making.

Colonel Albert Jakeway, successor to Colonel Coles, has a number of vocal compositions to his name, and many arrangements. The first was the vocal transcription of his own march, 'The great call', with words by his colleague of training college days, Arch Wiggins. Later he wrote a number of selections, including 'The Omnipotent God', a great favourite in the late 1920s. One of the Colonel's outstanding vocal creations is 'Joyous Heart', an extended solo which is not published in *The Musical Salvationist* but was issued as No. 1 in a new series of festival solos.

The present Head of the Music Editorial Department, Lieut.-Colonel Ray Steadman-Allen, has already earned himself an imperishable place in Army musical history. Natural gifts have been harnessed to acquired scholarship, both factors marking him out as possibly the Movement's most prolific and successful composer.

Like Bramwell Coles, under whose direction he first became a member of the department, his first love was the brass band and, quite rarely, his first published compositions were couched in that idiom.

His songs, however, are plentiful and of superb quality. 'O lovely name' (words by Will Brand), published in 1948, paved the way for 'Come and dwell in me' (words by Charles Wesley), 'Love's baptizing' (words by Albert Orsborn) and the more recent 'Remember me' (words by Isaac Watts). His arrangements of 'O save me, dear Lord', 'Take up thy cross' and 'I know Thee who Thou art' have added a new dimension to such songs and 'Blessed be the Lord my Strength' confirms his versatility.

His vocal *pièce de résistance* to date is undoubtedly 'We believe', written at the request of General Arnold Brown for use by the 1,000-voice chorus at the 1978 International Congress. One of the four centenaries celebrated at the Congress was that of the Salvation Army doctrines, and it was fitting that this should be commemorated with a setting of the Articles of Faith.

The Colonel has the rare gift of being able to produce not only the majestic anthem and miniature oratorio, but the simple emotional melody as well. 'Esher' and 'Blacklands' are examples.

The Assistant Head of the International Music Editorial Department, Major Leslie Condon, has written the music for many lovely songs. 'A song of praise' (words by Catherine Baird) had a place in the centenary festivals and there are a number of songs to his credit in succeeding issues of *The Musical Salvationist*. In his years as National Bandmaster and National Secretary for Bands and Songster Brigades he was required to provide numerous arrangements for united choruses to sing. 'All loves excelling' was among the most successful of these.

Former members of the department, Bandmasters Donald Osgood and Michael Kenyon, can be numbered among the consistent composers of vocal music, as can Retired Bandmaster Philip B. Catelinet, who, after a long period in musical professional work in the United States, is now resident in England. His music to 'I have joined the Army of the Lord' (words by Herbert Booth) dates back to his cadetship in the 'Awakeners' session when it was written for the weekly Thursday night march to Camberwell for the central holiness meeting. This melody caught on; Herbert Booth's original music had long been forgotten.

General Wilfred Kitching was the third generation of his family to contribute to *The Musical Salvationist*. His Quaker grandfather, William Kitching, was the writer of ' "Who comes to Me", the Saviour said', a much-used song in the Army song book, and it was to his sets of words that young Wilfred composed two melodies, both of which were published before his sixteenth birthday.

Commissioner Theodore Kitching, the General's father, was also the writer of several songs, the best known being 'How wonderful it is to walk with God'.

When General Kitching was a cadet, a training college officer was Adjutant Albert Orsborn. The poet and composer got together and this resulted in the birth of a number of songs, including 'I give Thee my best', 'In Him abiding' and 'I have cast my burden on the Saviour'. Among the General's many other vocal compositions published in *The Musical Salvationist* are 'Jesus, the very thought of

Thee', 'Toward the mark' and the popular solo 'Happy am I', the words of the last two being written by Lieut.-Commissioner Wiggins, his Lieutenant in the early years of officership.

Another able composer with whom the future General Orsborn joined forces in those days was Ensign (later Colonel) Albert Dalziel. His gift as a creator of lovely melodies was greatly respected and the added endowment of harmonic taste is proved in 'The Old Wells' and 'Jesu, O Jesu'.

Seven of the Army's eleven Generals have contributed to *The Musical Salvationist.* General Frederick Coutts was the author of two sessional songs while he was the Training Principal at Denmark Hill. The present international leader, General Arnold Brown, has written music and words through the years, providing both for 'I believe', a positive statement of faith, and the words only for 'The riches of His grace'. Bramwell Coles wrote the music to the last-named song.

A writer of useful words, Thomas Jackson, of Boston, Lincolnshire, gave valued service in the early decades of the century by providing lyrics for band marches. Two of the most popular of this group were 'The flowing river' and 'The land of happiness'. Another, 'The Life-saving guard's chanty', was a vocal setting of Brigadier William Broughton's march, 'Fighting Soldiers'.

The spectacular arrangements of Major Norman Bearcroft, National Secretary for Bands and Songster Brigades in the British Territory, require no recommendation. Beginning this form of composition when he was National Bandmaster, the many big national occasions during the 1960s provided him with ample scope for his undoubted ability. Aided by fanfare trumpets, full band, organ and other original effects, many an old song became rejuvenated in his skilful hands.

'With the conquering Son of God', 'Storm the forts' and a new garb for Leidzén's 'Homeward Bound' became familiar in Britain and later in Canada, when Major Bearcroft became Music Secretary in that territory.

In many events in Britain Norman Bearcroft was associated with Colonel Dean Goffin, then National Secretary for Bands and Songster Brigades, and the Colonel left a deep imprint upon the vocal life of the British Territory when he returned to his homeland, New Zealand, in 1966.

His arrangement of 'O boundless salvation' is still in constant use, and among his vocal music 'Hear me when I pray, my Father' and 'O be saved' (an arrangement) must have prominent place.

The musical offerings of Lieut.-Colonel Wesley Evans and Songster Leader Herbert Young, of Portland, must be included. Both have written material of worth over a long period of years, the Colonel being especially remembered for 'O Lamb of God' and the Songster Leader for 'Even me'.

Vocal compositions from all parts of the world make their way to London and, when published, wing their way to all of the eighty-two countries in which the Army flag flies. They are translated into many languages. Such territories have always had their own songwriters. Tribute is paid to Commissioner Richard Holz, Colonel William Maltby, Lieut.-Colonel Stanley Ditmer, Bruce Broughton and Envoy Tom Ferguson (USA); Allan Pengilly and Colonel Herbert Wallace (Australia); Bandmaster Thomas Rive (New Zealand); Brigadier Richard Nuttall (India); Colonel Kenneth Rawlins and Lieut.-Colonel Ernest Parr (Canada); Brigadier Lily Sampson (Australia), and a host of others.

It is hoped that omissions in such a mammoth task will be excused—if not forgiven!

Though he makes no mention of his own fine contribution, the name of Colonel Brindley Boon, author of this book, will forever be associated with Salvation Army music and song. Songs from his pen are sung all over the Salvation Army world and have already been acknowledged as classics of their kind. 'I would be Thy holy temple' and 'Spirit Divine' are but two of these. In the record of Salvation Army songwriters he bears an illustrious name.

Literary Secretary.

CHAPTER SEVENTEEN

ROBBING THE DEVIL

IF William Booth did not actually say, 'Why should the devil have all the best tunes?' he came very close to it on several occasions. *The Bandsman and Songster* in 1921 gave John Wesley the credit for the much-quoted statement but extensive search in his diaries has failed to confirm this fact.

In wishing readers of *The War Cry* 'a merry Christmas' in 1880, the Founder again made his ideas unmistakably clear. 'Music is to the soul what wind is to the ship', he declared, 'blowing her onwards in the direction in which she is steered. . . . Not allowed to sing that tune or this tune? Indeed! Secular music, do you say? Belongs to the devil, does it? Well, if it did, I would plunder him of it, for he has no right to a single note of the whole gamut. He's the thief! . . . Every note and every strain and every harmony is divine and belongs to us'.

James Dowdle, when addressing the 1877 annual conference of The Christian Mission and commenting upon Booth's lengthy discourse on 'good singing!', revealed that the first time he had seen William Booth in Whitechapel ten years earlier he was singing 'O how I love Jesus' to the tune of 'In and out the window', an adaptation of 'So early in the morning'.

The pioneer songs handed down from successful revival campaigns eventually gave way to words written to national melodies. A song published in the first issue of *The War Cry* at the end of 1879 gave the tune as 'The Red, White and Blue'. Queen Victoria had been on the throne for forty-two years and England was in the throes of an era of complacent if ebullient jingoism.

In time popular sentimental ballads became the order of the day and then downright comic song tunes. William Booth did not approve.

The first recorded use of a melody of this kind occurred during a visit by the Founder to Worcester in February 1882. 'Sailor' Fielder, who had been the second cadet to enter the Devonshire Road training home for men two years before, sang a new song by Captain William Baugh. This had been published in *The War Cry* two months before and was written to a music hall hit of the day, 'Champagne Charlie'. The solo, 'Bless His name He sets me free', was enthusiastically received, the congregation joining heartily in the refrain again and again. The General was not overjoyed.

Two weeks later he conducted a council of war at Bristol. In the Monday afternoon meeting, and again at night, the converted sea captain was called upon to repeat his solo. Some of the Army's generous supporters were not convinced as to the wisdom or taste of the radical departure. They strongly protested to William Booth and threatened to withdraw their financial backing should he allow the practice to continue.

The Founder was obviously worried. There could be no doubt that the song he had heard, and others, were successes. Despite his personal misgivings and long-held resentment to this kind of worship, he had to face facts. But could he afford to forego the help of his influential friends?

He decided to put the experiment to the test. The occasion was the opening of the Clapton Congress Hall in May 1882, when a galaxy of non-Salvationist stars was present.

Captain Gipsy Smith was there to sing James Bateman's 'The Blood of Jesus cleanses white as snow' to the tune 'I traced her little footsteps in the snow'; Adelaide Cox was brought from service in France to sing 'If you want pardon, if you want peace' written by George P. Ewens, first editor of *The War Cry*, to 'Pretty Louise'; and 'Sailor' Fielder sang the converted version of 'Champagne Charlie'.

It is not known if the soloists realized they were on trial, but they sang their hearts out while the General and his leading officers awaited the reaction. The large congregation was soon carried away. Choruses were repeated again and again and gradually the public resentment weakened until everyone was clapping hands in rhythm with the songs and waving handkerchiefs.

In this unexpected way hand-clapping was first introduced into Army meetings and the battle for the 'devil's tunes' was won.

At the psychological moment in the meeting the General stepped forward, told the audience how much it had cost to transform the London Orphanage into the National Training Barracks and appealed for a good collection. The response on that spring afternoon nearly 100 years ago was £4,300. 'They're pelting me with gold!' cried the Founder as they threw their sovereigns on to the platform.

Who were those three men who first wrested melodies from the devil's grasp and gave them new life and new meaning?

Before conversion James Bateman was a heavy-drinking music hall performer. He was an acceptable singer and a good banjo player. After his evening turn on the boards he would retire to the nearest public house, sing some more songs and go round with the hat to gather more money for more beer.

One of the songs Bateman sang was 'I traced her little footsteps in the snow'. It was surely the most natural thing in the world that when Bateman got saved he should want to get his songs saved as well.

One night, when he left the bar to join a Salvation Army meeting being held outside the premises, intent on mock participation, the Lord spoke to him. This resulted in his glorious conversion. His songs took on a new look, and 'I traced her little footsteps' quickly became 'The Blood of Jesus cleanses white as snow'.

'Lottie Lane' became 'Sinner, see yon light'; 'Under the Union Jack' became 'Under the Blood and Fire Flag'; 'Sailing, sailing' was transformed into 'Fighting, fighting on the narrow way'; and in addition God gave him melodies to put to his own words. These included 'Calvary's stream is flowing'; 'Down where the living waters flow' and 'The day of victory's coming'.

His last completed song was 'Joy without alloy'. As a Captain he was promoted to Glory in 1888, having commanded some of the Army's largest corps, among them Leicester, Hanley and Clapton Congress Hall.

George Phippen Ewens had a very different background, although his father did plunge the family into misery through his excessive drinking habits. The boy's maternal grandfather was at one time the Mayor of Glastonbury and one of the last private owners of the famous ruins.

A printer by trade and possessing certificates signed by Isaac Pitman for shorthand (a teacher's diploma) and advanced Spanish, he came under the influence of The Christian Mission when he was thirty years of age and, although he was married with a small family, did not hesitate when William Booth enlisted his help at headquarters.

His familiar pen-name, based on his initials, revealed his deep spiritual character. It was 'Grace, Peace, Evermore'. He was the first Salvationist to have a song published with both words and music. This was 'The Hallelujah Fountain'.

The third of the trio was William Baugh. He was the Commanding Officer at Regent Hall when 'Champagne Charlie' was 'converted'. Previously he was stationed at Whitechapel where Charles Jeffries, leader of the 'Skeleton Army', was one of his converts.

During the Captain's stay at Regent Hall the daughter of a peer knelt at the Mercy Seat. It was difficult for her to claim victory. There were so many questions to be answered. The officer tried to help her, but it was still a struggle. Later, those questions and his answers were expressed in song form, 'Why should I be a slave to sin?' now in *The Song Book of The Salvation Army*.

William Baugh is also associated with another converted secular melody. In 1887 a male cadet took a piece of music to the Music Department, then at Clapton, and said to Richard Slater, 'I have a tune I think would be of use to you'. The song was 'Minnie, darling, come and wander'.

Slater agreed it was a good tune, and placed it in a file for future reference. He also kept a file for suitable words to be 'married' to unclaimed music. One day a copy of the Canadian *War Cry* arrived containing a set of words by Captain Baugh, who was then serving in that country. The words were cut out and placed in the scrapbook as likely to be of service.

'Later', remembered Slater, 'I was going over the stock of materials and came across the tune from Australia and the words from Canada. They agreed in an admirable way for a song. They were then and there united "in holy matrimony" and have lived together ever since in happy union'. This was 'Blessed Saviour, now behold me' with the refrain, 'Breathe upon me'.

With Army names given to melodies in the tune book it is not easy to recognize the original settings. In fact, recent generations of Salvationists are not aware of the secular origins of tunes they imagine have always belonged to the Army.

'And above the rest' was originally 'Buffalo Gals'. 'O wash me now' once had the words, 'Come sister dear, kiss me goodnight' associated with it. 'It was on the Cross' was 'The Sailor's Grave'. 'In evil long I took delight' is a religious version of:

> Just down the lane,
> There by the stile
> Under the old oak tree;
> The clock strikes nine,
> There you will find
> Somebody waiting for me.

'Then carry me back to Tennessee' became 'The Judgment Day'; 'Down in a green and shady bed a modest violet grew' was reformed into 'Ten thousand souls', and it is well known that 'Storm the forts of darkness' was once 'Come, landlord, fill the flowing bowl'.

Charles Fry's most famous song, 'I've found a Friend in Jesus' ('He's the Lily of the Valley') was written to the melody of 'The little old log cabin down the lane', and he also converted 'Ever of thee I'm fondly dreaming' into 'Farewell to thee, vain world' and 'We have lived and loved together' into 'I have loved and lived with Jesus'.

Even some hymn tunes have non-religious backgrounds. 'Irish' is one in point. The words originally associated with this tune were:

> There was a Cameronian cat,
>   Was hunting for a prey,
> And in the house she catched a mouse
> Upon the Sabbath day.

The value of Stephen Foster's plaintive melodies was early realized. Herbert Booth wrote, 'O what battles I've been in' ('Poor old Uncle Ned'); 'Joy, freedom, peace' ('Old folks at home') and 'Gone are the days of wretchedness and sin' ('Poor old Joe'). He also turned the Negro spiritual 'O dem golden slippers' into 'O the blessed Lord'.

The outstanding exponent of the conversion of secular melodies to Army use was, is and ever will be Albert Orsborn. The 'will be' is included because stringent copyright laws now prohibit 'robbing the devil' to continue. 'It was not my natural bent to write sacred words to secular tunes', said General Orsborn in his autobiography. 'Left to myself I would never have done it. In that case my life would have missed one of its widest and most rewarding opportunities.'

The General began the habit as a young officer on the training college staff. He was required to produce a song a week for the great holiness meetings held in the Clapton Congress Hall. He too, as the soloist, introduced the song and was expected to make the vast crowd take up the chorus.

This pattern was begun in 1912 and the output was maintained for three years. As war songs began to be sung and heard, these popular hits were pressed into commission week by week at Clapton. No music was published and no titles were given. The public knowledge of the tunes was relied upon and excellent pianists in Wilfred Kitching and Albert Dalziel were on hand to provide improvised accompaniments.

In this way, and at this time, 'It's a long way to Tipperary' became 'On the ocean of love and mercy'; 'There's a long, long trail awinding' became 'It's a long, hard road to Calvary'; 'Love's old sweet song' was transformed into 'Sacred hands of Jesus'; and the 'Pink Lady' waltz, ('Dance, pretty lady') was converted into 'Let the beauty of Jesus be seen in me'.

Another radical change was 'We parted on the shore' to 'We're in the Father's care'. These new words were written during the first weekend after the outbreak of war in 1914. This, in its original version, was one of the many successes of Sir Harry Lauder.

Years before, the great little Scot had wooed and won a Salvation Army girl. This led him, it is said, to write his famous war-time song, 'I love a lassie'. Years later, an Army girl, selling her copies of *The War Cry,* entered his hotel. Sir Harry, for the price of a generous

donation, asked to borrow the girl's bonnet for only a few minutes.
Returning it, he explained he had asked his wife to put it on, that he
might see her as she was 'when we were first acquaint'.

'After that', says General Orsborn, 'I had no qualms about giving
Harry's melodies the free publicity of our usage'. Other Lauder songs
suitably reclothed in a salvation cloak by Albert Orsborn are 'Inver-
arary' ('Forth to rescue the dying') and 'Roamin' in the gloamin''
'Onward, ever onward, with a spirit true and bright').

Other secular melodies to be renewed in the hands of this master
of transformation were 'The vacant chair' ('In the secret of Thy
presence'); 'The old rustic bridge' ('Except I am moved with com-
passion'); 'Mother Machree' ('The charm of the Cross') and 'The voice
in the old village choir' ('The well is deep and I require a draught of
the water of life'). He even turned a theme from Sir Arthur
Sullivan's 'Iolanthe' into 'Spirit of love, come and in me reside'.

This practice did, of course, work in reverse. In the early days the
roughs followed the processions, singing parodies of Army songs.
'Glory to His name' was used frequently, the middle couplet being
altered to:

>Stick to my heart
>Like a penny jam tart!

These and similar parodies were sometimes attributed to
Salvationists themselves!

One of the most blatant parodies was included in the musical
show, 'The Belle of New York', a late 1890 Broadway production
based upon the life of an Army girl. At one stage the chorus was
required to sing:

>The bells of hell go ding-a-ling-a-ling
> For you but not for me;
>On high the angels sing-a-ling-a-ling,
>   That's where I'm going to be,
>O death, where is thy sting-a-ling-a-ling,
>   O grave thy victory?
>No ding-a-ling-a-ling, no sting-a-ling-a-ling
> But sing-a-ling-a-ling for me.

It is fitting that Albert Orsborn should have the last word in this
chapter which pays tribute to his genius.

'If we gave a song a different meaning, it was like giving a lovely
lady a new dress. Everyone was the better for it. Incidentally, this
thing was done with folk songs, in other religious communities, long
before we thought of it. Most songs of the ballad type are—or were—
so near to Salvation Army metres and melodies that no violence was
needed to convert them.'

CHAPTER EIGHTEEN

MEMORABLE MILESTONES

IT was a bold venture of faith that led William Booth, in 1890, to take the Crystal Palace for a salvation field day. The Founder was determined that the Army would celebrate its twenty-fifth anniversary in right royal style and the crowds attended in their tens of thousands. A feature of the day was the musical festival defined on the programme as 'The Battle of Song'. Herbert Booth, Commandant for Britain, was the maestro.

The huge orchestra was a phalanx of faces. Around the conductor, on the lower seats, were the massed string bands, under the direction of Richard Slater. Next in ascending order were the members of the Household Troops and Home Office Bands with Bandmaster Harry Appleby in charge. Behind the bands were ranged the first company of singers, 500 in number, each carrying a tambourine, the sound and sight of which in action was likened by Herbert to the 'rattle and glitter of a steel-clad battalion doing musical drill'.

Up and beyond these was the main body of singers—to the left 1,200 male officers, each man clad in a red jersey and holding in his hand a fluttering flag. On the right there was a corresponding company of female officers, each lass robed in the sombre uniform of bonnet and dark blue, and each holding one of the many coloured pennants.

Above the great chorus, fringing the semi-circle at the top, was the junior chorus, 500 girls ranged above the women and 500 boys above the men. Each youngster held a flag, making another brilliant scene of colour. Fred Fry was at the organ.

At a signal from Herbert Booth, Fry struck the keys of the grand organ, the women singers removed their sashes, then their bonnets, and suddenly the sashes were seen to stretch out into broad folds of pure white, the colourful effect strongly contrasting with the flame-red jerseys of the men.

The audience of some 15,000 people sat spellbound as, in response to the conductor's baton, that mighty chorus thundered forth Herbert Booth's music to William Pearson's words, 'God is keeping His soldiers fighting . . . but we're sure to have the victory'.

Such a spectacular display and volume of song had never before been seen or heard at the Crystal Palace. Dr Robertson Nicoll, an eminent preacher of the day, exclaimed excitedly to an interviewer: 'Man, the Army is made, but it will have to go wary and not lose its head and become great in its own conceit'.

A few days later, speaking to officers in council and referring to the celebrations, the General said: 'Comparisons are always tricky, but we are bound to give my son [Herbert] our homage today for his remarkable gift displayed last Tuesday. His management revealed a talent for that sort of thing that will be invaluable to the Army in the future.'

All this was eight years before the first songster brigade was officially recognized. This was the beginning of a long history of united singing that has culminated with four different choruses of a thousand voices doing duty at the Royal Albert Hall and Wembley during the 1978 International Congress.

The congresses of 1886, 1894 and 1904 had their share of happy vocal expression. There were no visiting brigades as such, but the delegates sang songs typical of their respective countries and brought their own distinctive culture to the proceedings.

In 1894, for instance, the American delegates, under the leadership of Ballington Booth, featured a song which he had written for the occasion. This was 'Over and over, like a mighty sea'. It was a hit. Other delegations took it up, and soon audiences at every event were swaying to the rhythm of this attractive waltz-like chorus. Salvationists, with their flair for spontaneous inventiveness, soon discovered that another chorus, 'Over the sea . . . Jesus Saviour pilot me' fitted with it. Much later, as if to preserve the nautical flavour, 'My bonnie lies over the ocean' was added, all three choruses going at the same time. It must be explained that the original words of the third refrain were substituted with 'God's love . . . is sufficient for me'.

In 1904 the 'Yankee Choir' made a great appeal.

By the time the 1914 Congress arrived things were very different. The development of organized singing had spread to many territories and many groups made their way to London for the celebrations.

Singing brigades from Switzerland, Finland, Holland, Denmark and Norway represented Europe, and the American coloured vocalists were there to sing 'Goodbye, Pharaoh', 'Roll along Jordan' and other such songs written by one of their number, Envoy Tom Ferguson. The contribution of the West Indian Singers has been highlighted in an earlier chapter.

The International Staff Songsters sang an unpublished piece by Major Goldsmith (music) and Ensign Orsborn (words) entitled 'Our faithful Lord'.

The Congress was overshadowed before it began by the *Empress of Ireland* tragedy which carried 133 Salvationists to their watery death. At the memorial service, held in the Royal Albert Hall, the meeting began with the entrance down the aisle in single file of members of the International Staff Songsters, Salvation Singers and Brixton Songster Brigade. As they slowly walked in step they sang 'Rock of ages' to the tune of 'Bath Abbey'.

The first record of united songsters taking part in a festival after the 1st World War was in January 1921. The occasion was the Bandmasters' Councils festival and the pieces sung, under the leadership of Lieut.-Colonel Herbert Jackson, were 'Since Jesus came into my heart' and 'The Homeward Trail'.

In 1927 the first composers' festival was held at the Clapton Congress Hall, but songwriters were not represented, nor did any vocal section take part. The following year, in the presence of the Duke and Duchess of York (later King George VI and Queen Elizabeth), amends were made when Major Charles Coller conducted the united songsters in 'Jesus said: "I am the resurrection and the life"' and Songster Leader Oliver Cooke led them in 'I know a fount'.

The songwriters, with the composers of band music taking part, were presented to their Royal Highnesses. The composers' festival at the Wembley Pool on the penultimate day of the 1978 Congress was planned to mark the golden jubilee of that event.

Toward the end of 1928 it was announced that the British Commissioner (Commissioner Samuel Hurren) would conduct songster councils at the Mildmay Conference Centre, Newington Green, on a Sunday in the following January. It was admitted that some songsters felt that they had been left out 'in the cold'. It was hoped that with this innovation they would feel very much 'in the warm'.

The promised councils did not materialize, although in January 1929 the first National Songster Festival took place at Clapton Congress Hall. These events became popular, especially in the exciting 1930s, and continued to be held regularly in the same historic hall until 1969, exactly forty years after the first.

That final festival was a nostalgic occasion. Something of the old-time spirit was recaptured as the massed songsters, with Major Leslie Condon as soloist, featured a medley of early-day song-hits. The Major's costume, red jersey and pillbox hat, added a touch of authenticity.

The Army vacated the premises early the following year and there has never been a venue that has adequately replaced this majestic hall of hallowed memories. Much of the building is demolished but the impressive frontage has been retained. It stands as a 'Greek ruin' amid trees and lawns to form a focus of a classical vista next to a rebuilt school.

In 1971 the National Songster Festival was taken north to the Sheffield City Hall and a year later, again to the provinces, to Birmingham Town Hall. More recent events have been housed in the Westminster Central Hall (1975) and the Royal Festival Hall (1977).

The 1934 festival demands a special mention because of an unusual and regrettable happening. For some inexplicable reason, perhaps unique in Army history, a double quantity of tickets was printed and issued. On the night, people arriving at Clapton were surprised, amazed and then irate to find that their seats were occupied. Total chaos reigned for a long time but in the end common sense prevailed.

The records show that that was the Congress Hall's biggest crowd. They do not explain that most of the seats had two occupants!

When the 'Torchbearers' Session of cadets was commissioned as officers in May 1933 thirty of the men and twenty-six of the women were selected for special service. These were to be known as the Musical Troopers and Musical Miriams.

Following the example of their famous predecessors, the Household Troopers of 1887, the bandsmen, wearing capes and helmets, were to cover 500 miles on foot. The leader was Brigadier Handel Boot; the Bandmaster, Captain Edward Saywell, and the Deputy Bandmaster, Captain Bernard Adams.

The Miriams, led by Major Frances Barker and Captain Dorothy Gamgee, would travel 1,000 miles 'blazing the salvation trail' in a 'motor chariot'.

After a farewell meeting at Clapton the young officers marched down Linscott Road, amidst scenes of tremendous excitement, to take their respective ways. At least, the Troopers marched; the Miriams rode triumphantly in their chariot, waving their tambourines from the open windows. They too wore helmets.

For the women Lieutenants the first stop was Chalk Farm, where a meeting was held and where they billeted for the night. Early next morning they were away, their campaign covering eleven counties in the Midlands and North of England. A combined welcome meeting in August greeted the united warriors.

The first councils exclusively for songsters were held in the Clapton Congress Hall in January 1934 under the leadership of the British Commissioner (Commissioner Charles Jeffries). This was evidence, suggested *The Bandsman and Songster*, 'of the growing importance of our songster brigades and the influence they may exercise in the ex-

CHAPTER NINETEEN

TREASURY OF PRINT

IT could not have been too long after the beginning of Christian Mission activity before William Booth felt the time had come to give urgent consideration to publishing a collection of suitable hymns. A series of home-produced leaflets containing words of some popular gospel songs had been in circulation for some time, but now came the great need for a more permanent production.

The Christian Mission Hymn Book—words only—compiled by 'the Rev. W. Booth' was the outcome. Said the preface: 'Our only apology for the introduction of another hymn book is that we have not found one containing a sufficient number of hymns suitable for the regular services of a congregation, and at the same time adapted to all the requirements of open-air and revival meetings.'

There were 531 hymns in this collection. Established classics of the Church were mixed with revival songs with expressive refrains. It was a comprehensive little volume, suited to all occasions.

Although the date of this publication cannot be accurately determined, it can confidently be supposed that it was before 1870. One of the pages gave the information that quantities could be obtained 'at a reduction from Mr Booth, 3 Gore Road, Victoria Park Road, London, who will send a single copy, post free, for the price in postage stamps'. The Booth family moved to this address just before Evangeline's birth in 1865 and it is apparent from the foregoing that these premises became the Mission's headquarters until the People's Market was purchased in 1870. The administration was then centred at this site in Whitechapel and remained there until the removal to Queen Victoria Street in 1881.

With later developments it was not unnatural that *The Christian Mission Hymn Book* should become the *Hallelujah Hymn Book*.

The first attempt to produce an independent book of tunes was in 1876. This was *Revival Music,* and in its publication William Booth's chief assistant was Mary Billups, a daughter of influential friends William and Catherine had met some thirteen years before while conducting a campaign in Cardiff. Mary came under the influence of Catherine Booth and entered their home as a paying guest in 1868. One of the attractions of this arrangement was that she could become a student at the London College of Music and thus fulfil a long-held ambition.

Commissioner Frederick Booth-Tucker described her as a 'gay, fashionable worldling, a brilliant musician'. Her conversion in a meeting led by Catherine Booth during a campaign at Margate led to her sacrificing the prospects of a musical and literary career to enter full-time service with the Mission. In the year *Revival Music* was published Mary Billups married a minister of religion named Irvine and settled with him in Canada.

Revival Music contained 494 tunes. In 1880 it was reissued as *Salvation Army Music* with thirty-nine more songs added. This enlarged publication was issued by Salvation Army Book Stores, Paternoster Row, close to St Paul's Cathedral.

Again William Booth's preface is worth quoting. 'It seems to me', he said, 'unnecessary to give reasons for the production of the present book, seeing that a cursory examination must convince anyone that it contains such a collection of popular revival melodies as has never before appeared, the majority of which have been proved to be unrivalled in adaptability and power to stir the hearts of the multitude.'

Above each tune was printed the number of the song as published in *The Christian Mission Hymn Book*. This intriguing cross-reference system was extended when *Salvation Army Songs* was published.

Numbers shown over the songs in this words-only version referred to the tune number in *Salvation Army Music*. All three references must have filled a real need.

Shortly before his death in 1926, Major George P. Ewens recalled for the benefit of *Bandsman and Songster* readers what the editor designated 'Genesis of Musical Department'. The recollections went back to about 1881.

One morning Ewens was walking from his home to the Whitechapel Headquarters when he met Miss Emma Booth. She greeted him with the news that she was bound for the same destination—with manuscripts for the 'General's Tune Book'. The young man asked if he might glance at the copies and was horrified to find that the prepared material was not at all suitable in that form. He offered to deliver the precious cargo to save Miss Emma the journey, and she agreed, after getting Ewens to promise to deliver the manuscripts personally to her father.

Later, in the General's office, Captain Ewens explained that the arrangements were not vocal enough and would need to be prepared in four-part harmony. Tunes in *Salvation Army Music* had appeared in that style and this pattern needed to be followed.

The General asked what he knew about the subject and Ewens began to speak of his interest and limited experience.

'That will do', interrupted the General. 'I am very busy, but before I go away take in this. We are making arrangements to start a musical department. We are simply swamped—everyone is either singing or playing an instrument. I have no time for details. I appoint you to take up matters *pro tem* and see this music book through for me. In the interim, if you are short of money, draw from the cashiers ten shillings per week by my authority. Do your best. God bless you!'

George Ewens became so engrossed in his unexpected involvement that he worked early and late. He forgot to apply to the cashiers. 'It was a labour of love', he reported.

This book was *Salvation Music Volume 2,* published in December 1883, two months after the Music Department had been set up at Clapton under the supervision of Herbert Booth, with Richard Slater in charge.

In his preface William Booth stated: 'The Salvation Army must always be singing new songs whilst it continues to win new victories. Old songs will not do where there is plenty of new life'. A list of thirty-five acknowledgments shows that, even at that early stage, the Army was observing the requirements of Copyright Law. He explained: 'We seize upon the strains that have already caught the ear of the masses, we load them with our one great theme—salvation—and so we make the very enemy help us to fill the air with our Saviour's fame'.

This slim, progressive volume of ninety-nine songs contained, for the first time, original material written by Salvationist authors and composers. On a page at the back was advertised the *Salvation Soldiers' Song Book,* known affectionately as the 'Penny Song Book'.

The next edition of *Salvation Army Songs* (words only) was published in 1899. General Booth spoke truly when he opened his preface with: 'Surely no man has ever been called upon to make, or direct the making of, so many song books as I have. It is no little consolation at seventy to know that millions of people in every part of the world are singing God's praises together as a result of the efforts He had helped me to put forth or to direct for their good.' As a companion to this book, bands were supplied with 303 tunes and for vocal purposes the keyboard edition, with words, was issued.

For the 1899 song book several people were asked to submit a collection of likely material. In an interview with the Founder on 3 November 1897, Brigadier Slater, the music editor, was requested to sift the songs received and recommend 2,500 for further consideration. To his amazement Slater was confronted with a pile of 11,000 songs. From this formidable collection he picked out the number required by the General, who in conference with some leading officers reduced the selection to 870.

In 1926 General Bramwell Booth set up a special commission known as the Song Book Council, to explore the possibility of a new song book. The first chairman was Colonel (later General) George Carpenter, and others to serve in this capacity were Commissioner Theodore Kitching and, during the final months, Colonel Herbert Jackson.

This resulted in the 1930 song book being published, a keyboard edition appearing in 1931. This was a words and music reproduction of the band tune book published in 1928—and still in use. Edward J. Higgins was the General at the time the new song book was issued.

It is perhaps fitting that 1978—the year of the fifth International Congress—should have marked the twenty-fifth anniversary of *The Song Book of The Salvation Army*. Inspired by the interest and encouragement of General Albert Orsborn, the Song Book Revision Council sought to produce a selection of established songs of the Church and of the Army, with many salvation gems which had been written since the turn of the century added. The council's two chairmen were Commissioner William Dalziel and Colonel Bramwell Coles.

Supplementary tune books have appeared since, completing an impressive treasury of music in print. *Keep Singing!*, a publication of 102 songs with identical numbers for words-only and music editions, was published in 1976 by authority of General Clarence Wiseman.

It has already been recorded that the duties of the first members of the Music Editorial Department included participation in the campaigns conducted by training home cadets led by Commandant Herbert Booth and his sisters, Emma and Eva, and writing songs for their use. This resulted in the publication of *Favourite Songs of the Salvation Songsters* and later *Favourite Songs of the Speaking, Singing and Praying Brigade*.

There was still a growing need for more vocal material. The first International Congress of 1886 brought a flood of new songs from all parts of the world and Slater was busy throughout with his note-book and pencil. This resulted in *The Musical Salvationist* being published in July of that year, two months after the congress. This magazine has appeared regularly ever since, and from 1961 in its enlarged, covered format. Tonic sol-fa was introduced with the old notation in 1891 and ceased a few years ago.

In 1922 popular 'repeats' began to be printed. The first publication was *Gems for Songsters No. 1*. This immediate success was followed by *Gems No. 2* (1924); *Gems No. 3* (1936), and four more in the series at intervals. *Revival Songs* No. 1, 2 and 3 have also appeared, as have *Songs for Male Voices* (the first in 1922), *Songs for Women's Voices* (1931) and *Songs for Home Leagues* (1955). *The Young People's Song Book* was published in 1963.

The Salvationist Soloist No. 1 was issued in 1922, with a foreword by General Bramwell Booth. This words and melody publication contained a varied selection of *Musical Salvationist* successes spanning a period of more than thirty years. If some of these, like their writers, have passed into Army music history, others have received a breath of new life by being included in band compositions.

Another words and melody production which immediately became popular was *The Salvation Army Chorus Book,* published in November 1945. In the preface General Carpenter says: 'This collection will do much to keep in use choruses which might otherwise be forgotten. Let us sing them, old and new, to the glory of God!'

A feature of early day issues of *The Musical Salvationist* was the printing of a companion words-only version. These were produced in two booklets, the first to cover volumes 1 to 9, and the second to correspond with volumes 10 to 12, the latter published in 1899. It was not unusual when songster brigades sang such songs for the congregation to follow the words from the special books. The International Staff Songsters favoured this in their meetings.

Two editions of *The Salvation Soloist* published in Melbourne, one in 1911, the other in 1918, have had long and useful lives, and these, with words and melody only, bear a strong resemblance to their counterparts issued in London. The Australasian version came out first.

While the majority of territories use *The Song Book of The Salvation Army,* it is necessary for non-English-speaking countries to have their own production. Such localized activity in the matter of translating, composing, arranging, editing and printing, reveals the wealth of The Salvation Army's international resources.

The *USA Salvation Army Song Book* contains the songs of the international edition plus a supplement of words and music. An interesting fact is that some contributions published in London as words only are required in America to appear with music because of copyright restrictions in force on that side of the Atlantic Ocean.

A popular publication is *Songs of Faith,* published in Canada in 1971. This was made up of North American gospel songs and other material which was not included in the 1953 song book.

The needs of missionary countries have not been overlooked. In 1923 Commissioner Frederick Booth-Tucker issued a book of fifty-one Oriental songs gathered from all parts of India. The Commissioner, in his preface, expressed his thanks to Brigadiers Hawkes and Goldsmith for the 'useful harmonizing and arranging of the tunes', and explained that the purpose of the collection was, amongst other things, to assist officers on their first arrival in the East.

In 1966 the Music Editorial Department prepared for the Missionary Literature Section at International Headquarters a Tonic sol-fa tune book for use in developing areas of the world.

One of the responsibilities of the International Music Editorial Department is to discover and encourage new writers. This has sometimes been done by means of composers' and songwriters' competitions. The first of these was held in 1905 and the main section was for new melodies to old words. The then Staff-Captain Arthur Goldsmith secured first prize with his music to 'We're travelling home to heaven above', which at the time of its inclusion in the tune book supplement became 'Goldsmith'. Adjutant Charles Coller was another successful entrant, as was Songster Leader Oliver Cooke and Bandmaster Herbert Twitchin.

After a period of some years a National Music Competition for vocal compositions was announced in 1930, open to all Salvationists resident in the United Kingdom. There were 205 entries. First place in section 1 went to Songster Leader Cyril Piper, of Spennymoor, with 'Fear thou not'. In section 2 Bandmaster and Mrs Herbert Mountain, of Sheffield Citadel, were successful with 'Wonderful Promises' (this husband and wife team also secured second place, but in view of the rules could not receive an award, which went to Songster Leader J. W. Smith, of Bulwell). Both first prizes in the other sections went to Major Coller, and another name in the list, with a third prize, was Songster Leader Alfred Vickery, of Thornton Heath. He had already made a name for himself with 'Keep in step' and 'Ready for the fray' and was later to enhance his reputation with a series of sunshine songs, of which 'Travel along in the sunshine' is the best known.

So successful was this venture, and so widespread the publicity that, in response to overseas territories, a year later an international competition was announced. Amidst great excitement the winners' names were revealed from a sealed envelope at the National Songster Festival in January 1933, when first prize pieces received their first performances by brigades which had been required to rehearse a number of entries without knowing the successful one or the identity of the writer.

The response was truly international. Major Kristian Fristrup, of the USA, secured four prizes, two of them firsts. Others in the list were Sergeant J. H. Morgan, of Sydney (Australia); Bandmaster Cecil Greig, of Norwood (Australia); Captain Gordon Blake and Envoy

Susan Barker, of Victoria (Australia); Ensign Gösta Blomberg, of Stockholm (Sweden); and Bandmaster A. W. Millard, of Dunedin (New Zealand).

Veteran songwriter Alec Greig, of Aberdeen, appeared in the list, providing words to music composed by his son, Cecil, and among pieces that were successful in this competition were 'Song of Songs' (Adjutant Ernest Rance); 'The call to praise' (Songster Henry Kniveton and Staff-Captain Arch R. Wiggins); 'Happy am I' (Major Wilfred Kitching and Staff-Captain Wiggins); and 'The Seasons', a singing company song by Bandsman Charles Robinson, of Kilmarnock, who later became a member of the Music Editorial Department and is now Bandmaster at Leytonstone.

Two months after the festival yet another similar international competition was announced, on the same pattern, the results being announced publicly in the same way, at the National Songster Festival in January 1934.

Major Fristrup had four more successes to his credit; Cyril Piper, by this time Young People's Sergeant-Major at Southall, repeated his achievement of two years before with a selection, 'The Lord is my Rock'; Major Coller, Adjutant Rance (this time in collaboration with Adjutant Doris Rendell), the Greig father and son, the then Ensign Blomberg were again among the honours, together with a new writer, Bandsman Charles Skinner, of Bishop's Stortford.

Many songs of the three competitions lived and are still favourites on many songster programmes. Those events inspired many a hesitant writer to pit his skills, and the Music Editorial Department was enabled to build up a stock of material.

There have never been other competitions on this scale. They remain an indelible memory in the minds of those who were brought up in London between the wars and were privileged to attend those exciting festivals at Clapton Congress Hall, with their elements of surprise and thrills of hero worship.

CHAPTER TWENTY

DEVOTION AND DISCIPLINE

IN *No Discharge in This War,* General Frederick Coutts points out that Salvation Army songsters, like the bandsmen, are all pledged Salvationists—and of course unpaid. He goes on to make the point: 'Perhaps they are both among the select company of genuine amateurs still left in the field of leisure pursuits.'

The devotion of Army musicians is the envy of their secular counterparts. Rules and regulations laid down for the guidance of songsters are comparable to those of bandsmen. Apart from the 'no payment' aspect, the musicians are required to subscribe to the maintenance of their section and to buy uniforms duly trimmed with the design decided by the leaders and approved by Headquarters.

Uniformity of dress for songsters was not generally observed until some twelve years after the formation of the first offical brigades. This move was initiated by the Chief of the Staff, Bramwell Booth, in 1910. He was conducting annual councils for bandmasters, deputy bandmasters and songster leaders at Clapton in the January of that year and expressed a wish to meet the songster leaders 'over the tea cups' between the afternoon and evening sessions. He spoke to them of his delight with the improvement in the 'singing brigades' all over the country, and while they were moving in the right direction they had still a long way to go.

The Chief's suggestion that distinctive uniform for songsters was contemplated met with unanimous approval. Such a possibility was regarded as being a step in the right direction. The new design caught on, but not at once. In some cases it took years for a brigade to be fitted out in uniforms bearing the same regulation trimmings.

There can be no doubt that the early years of the Edwardian decade in England saw an advance in songster brigade interests. *The Bandsman and Songster* published a number of simple articles on the elements of the vocal art; the formation in which to sit for the best results; and how to teach a song. All this was necessary instruction to leaders who were pitchforked into vocal responsibility equipped only with brass-banding technique.

Such advice as the dangers of overeating for songsters was dealt with, as well as constant reminders of the spiritual implications of salvation singing.

At the councils of 1911, in which band sergeants were invited in place of deputy bandmasters, Bramwell Booth, in answer to a question submitted, stated that the matter of songster leaders wearing distinctive marks on their uniform was receiving attention. When these trimmings were eventually introduced the innovation was not welcomed by all bandmasters.

For many years the bandmaster had regarded himself—and been recognized by his superiors in many cases—as the music director of the corps, all other leaders being subservient to him. A few of them, when the new trimmings were introduced, would not permit the wearer to be so dressed when playing in the band. He was regarded as a bandsman who happened to be the songster leader.

Songster brigade discipline was undoubtedly retarded by the 1st World War. It was not until after the armistice that the promised distinctive design of songster uniform came into general use. In 1920, in fact.

It was announced: 'The songster brigade uniform which has recently been authorized is taking on immensely. Inquiries for the new designs are coming in at a rate that taxes the resources of the Women's Uniform Department to the utmost. The authorized designs are much admired, and the whole idea has proved itself exceedingly popular'.

The idea of discipline as already applied to bandsmen took time to 'sink in'. In 1921 a musical leader found it necessary to rebuke programme builders for 'un-Salvationizing', as he put it. This followed a reference to 'choir' instead of songster brigade, and 'Miss' in place of 'Songster'.

In January 1934 songster leaders were given a place on the corps census board and this was an imaginative and significant step. At last it gave them an equal voice with bandmasters in corps affairs and did away officially with the 'music director' tag. The songster reserve was introduced in 1951, to which songsters could be transferred after a reasonable length of service, to be called up when exigencies demanded.

One of the earliest regulations introduced was that insisting that only music published by The Salvation Army and issued from Headquarters should be sung. Many argue still that little suitable music is published and that they wish to use outside publications. How anyone can say that, after more than ninety years of *The Musical Salvationist*, is difficult to understand. Some of this music has been buried beneath the dust of history and is overdue for revival.

It becomes necessary from time to time for songster leaders, as well as bandmasters, to be reminded of the stringent copyright laws in existence in most countries of the world. The interests of authors and composers in Britain are vested in the Performing Rights Society, by whom fees are required. The regulation that only Army music shall be used is therefore a protection against the danger of infringing the law of the land and thereby committing not only a legal offence but a moral one as well.

Copyright law also covers the photocopying of printed music without permission from the owner of the copyright. This is a modern problem and one that requires to be closely watched.

These and other matters come within the administrative responsibility of the National Secretary for Bands and Songster Brigades. The manifold functions of the Bands Department appears in the companion to this volume, and something of the immensity of just one aspect of the curriculum is realized when, in sending out manuscript for the International Congress Chorus to rehearse, more than 90,000 sheets of foolscap paper were used. Every song had to be stapled and dispatched. Major Norman Bearcroft, National Secretary, was assisted in this gigantic task by the National Bandmaster (Captain Trevor Davis) and members of the diminutive staff.

Before composers and songwriters have a piece published they are required to complete an assignment form handing over their copyright to the General of The Salvation Army. This has not always been so, and came into force following an interesting incident.

In 1932, at a 'Day with God' meeting led by General Edward Higgins, the General recognized Gipsy Smith in the congregation. Gipsy had been one of the Founder's stalwarts in the Whitechapel days and served as an officer for some years. His last corps was Hanley and the reason for, and manner of, his leaving the ranks are well known. Gipsy Smith had settled in the United States and was internationally known as a gospel singer and revival campaign leader. The General invited him to the platform, where he received an overwhelming welcome and was given a few moments to speak. Before doing so he requested the congregation to sing 'my chorus'. He reminded them of the words, 'Let the beauty of Jesus be seen in me', and how the people sang in response to Gipsy's dynamic direction!

The chorus completed, the leader pointed out two slight errors in the notation they were singing and they tried again. The congregation gathered the impression that he had written the words.

Lieut.-Colonel (later General) Albert Orsborn, whom Salvationists have always recognized as the author of the chorus, was present in the meeting and afterwards met Gipsy to discuss the confusion. It was discovered that Gipsy Smith had used it for many years as his theme song; that it was the 'anthem' of Samuel Chadwick's Cliff College;

and that a Methodist revivalist actually printed it and held the copyright, with a slightly altered version of the music. This was the setting Gipsy tried to teach to a Salvationist congregation.

Furthermore, Gipsy Smith's biography was entitled *The Beauty of Jesus* and the words of the popular refrain were printed on the flyleaf. It will be remembered that General Orsborn's book of original poems carried the same title.

General Orsborn could provide no proof that he was the rightful author. In fact, a good case could have been made out against his claim. With possible legal complexities involving both the Army and the author, General Higgins quickly approved of recommendations that in future all contributors to Army music and songs would be required to give written confirmation that they were the composer of the music or author of the words, or both.

In addition, a signed undertaking would be given acknowledging that the copyright would become the property of The Salvation Army through the person of its General.

Since 1896 instrumental and vocal music supplied to Salvationist sections and soloists have been approved for publication by a Music Board. This group of officers was first called the International Headquarters' Music Board, with Commissioner John Carleton as chairman. Two years later the Commissioner became the Army's first songster leader. He remained chairman for twenty-five years.

Band and vocal music was presented to the board for approval, Major Richard Slater singing the songs to his colleagues while he accompanied himself at the organ. After a while, so that Slater might hear the new vocal compositions from a distance, his double duties were taken over by Major William Brindley Boon.

A few years before, the Major had been a Colonel and the Army's first Chief Secretary, serving under the leadership of Commandant Herbert Booth. He had resigned from the oversight of the International Trade Headquarters to devote himself to the advancement of various social and political reforms, but had returned not long afterwards with the rank of Adjutant, much disillusioned.

Earlier still, in his pre-Salvationist days, Major Boon had selected and edited *Tunes for Public Worship,* a companion to a hymn book published by the United Free Gospel Churches.

For many years the duties of presenting new vocal music to the board were shared by the International Staff Songsters and Salvation Singers. Only on special occasions were the full brigades used; mostly the responsibility was entrusted to smaller groups. Later the Assurance Songsters fulfilled the task.

The method of presentation has turned full circle. The present

Head of the International Music Editorial Department (Lieut.-Colonel Ray Steadman-Allen) plays the music on the piano to the International Music Board (Vocal) as his illustrious predecessor did eighty years ago.

While the four-part harmony, with occasional embellishments demanded on the copy, is played, members of the board follow the words, linking up the two. Today's chairman is Commissioner Harry Williams, who apart from being a doctor of medicine is an energetic music enthusiast.

Early in 1978, an emergency meeting of the board was called to hear the music editor's masterpiece, 'We believe'. As the final stanza was reached the chairman began to sing. Other members followed suit, self-consciously at first but with mounting courage as the full impact of the tremendous truths of the Army's doctrines was experienced.

Who is to say that that spontaneous outburst did not make history? It could well have done.

CHAPTER TWENTY-ONE

WITH HEART AND VOICE

SOLO singing was not featured a great deal in the earliest days of The Christian Mission. William Booth was wary of the slightest semblance of a personality cult. In later days he changed his mind and exploited solo singing with good effect. This does not mean that individual missioners were not permitted to express themselves in song. James Dowdle testified at the Mission's 1877 Council of War that when he first saw 'Mr Booth' he was singing. That initial encounter was in 1867. But it is evident that ten years later the idea had not completely caught on.

In the last chapter Gipsy Smith dramatically came into the story. He could have been the first recognized soloist of The Salvation Army. Having come under the influence of Evangelist William Corbridge, Rodney Smith (to give him his 'Sunday' name), who had been born in a gipsy tent in Epping Forest, attended a meeting led by William Booth at Whitechapel. Booth had been told of the seventeen-year-old lad's desire to become an evangelist in the mission and after several persons had addressed the meeting he said, 'The next speaker will be the gipsy boy'.

Smith records in his autobiography: 'There was only one gipsy boy in the meeting and I was he. My first inclination was to run away, but immediately the thought came to me that that would never do. . . . Trembling, I took my way to the platform and when I reached it I shook in every limb. Mr Booth, with that quick eye of his, saw that I was in something of a predicament and at once said, "Will you sing us a solo?" I said, "I will try, sir", and that night I sang my first solo at a big public meeting'.

In this unprepared way Gipsy Smith was launched on a career of singing evangelism that was to take him around the world on several occasions. His recordings of gospel songs in the developing days of the gramophone met with great success.

When the Mission became the Army there was an upsurge of solo singing. The new terminology, with emphasis on war, fighting and victory, lent itself to this and William Booth was among the first to realize the mighty potential of the human voice. He was quick to recognize those who, with heart and voice, could contribute vitally to a meeting.

One of these was Elinor Kelly, discovered by Herbert Booth when she was a member of his Speaking, Singing and Praying Brigade. The Founder used her regularly in his meetings until she was appointed to serve as a pioneer officer in Sweden. There, as Captain Kelly, she met and married Staff-Captain Erik Leidzén, becoming the mother of 'young Erik', born four months after his father's death whilst on a journey as Sweden's Territorial Young People's Secretary.

Another member of Herbert Booth's pioneer Salvation Songsters in the 1880s was Richard Adby. As a lad he was always singing and when the Army 'opened fire' in his native Buckinghamshire town of High Wycombe it was the singing in the open air that attracted him. At the time he was employed in one of the factories of the chair industry for which the town is famous. He was in great demand as a lunch-time entertainer and became a popular personality. After conversion he was one of the chief singers of the corps.

While a cadet, Adby was present one Thursday afternoon at a bombardment of Mile End Waste led by the Commandant. He was asked to sing, and he responded with 'Ere the sun goes down', a song he first brought into the Army and he was the first to sing it in the meetings.

In the crowd that afternoon was a man who, the following Sunday, arrived at Clapton Congress Hall and asked to see the young man who had sung 'Ere the sun goes down'. Adby was found and, kneeling beside the seeker for truth, all that he could get out of him was, 'I must get my sins forgiven ere the sun goes down'. At length the light of Heaven streamed into his soul and the assurance that he was saved from his sin came to him. God used him subsequently to lead his wife and daughter to the Saviour and he became the respected colour sergeant of a London corps.

Eliza Archer was employed at Peter Robinson's emporium in London's Oxford Circus. She had a beautiful voice and often sang to the girls in the workroom. One of them invited her to a meeting at Regent Hall, then recently opened, and she went 'for the fun of the thing'. Her knowledge of the secular tunes to which the congregational songs were sung made her feel quite at home, and she thoroughly enjoyed joining in, although she sang the original words. In a subsequent Friday night holiness meeting she knelt at the Penitent-form, influenced earlier by the singing of 'Who'll be the next to follow Jesus?' She was the first to accept the invitation on that occasion.

Sister Archer became a Salvationist and was frequently used in the meetings as a soloist. Her passionate singing of 'Not my own, but saved by Jesus', coupled with her glowing testimony, stirred the heart of the converted young infidel, Richard Slater, who was determined to win her affection. They were married on 17 September 1884, the wedding being the first to be conducted at Regent Hall. Many of Slater's first songs were featured as a solo by his wife.

Brigadier Tom Plant was one of the first Army specialists. The majority of Salvationists have been required to follow their musical interests and pursuits in addition to duties which had prior claim upon them. Early in his career as an officer, Tom Plant was appointed as a 'Musical Special' and as such conducted numerous campaigns in Britain and elsewhere over a period of some years.

He had already acquired considerable skill on the guitar, banjo, concertina and lute before becoming an officer in 1888, and he quickly added tubular bells and many instruments of his own invention and patent to the list. His quick wit, mischievous sense of humour and good singing voice added to the attraction, and he was in great demand.

The arrival of Tom Plant and his horse-drawn pantechnicon at a corps was an occasion. An army of small boys was usually on hand to help him unload, for which they were suitably rewarded with a bar of chocolate. After the meeting, which invariably concluded with a forthright message, spiritual appeal and seekers, there was the dismantling of equipment, loading up of the van and a few hours' rest for the singing evangelist before moving on.

One of the Brigadier's most popular attractions was his 'humaphone'. These could be purchased during the meeting in time for the first lesson from the master performer. One was required to hum into the weird contraption, which was designed to fit in metal mask fashion over the nose and mouth. Hence its name. After the initial stages of mucus embarrassment had been negotiated, varying degrees of efficiency were achieved. Humaphone bands were quite the rage for a while.

The gifted wandering minstrel wrote many songs, mostly for himself to sing and to meet the peculiar need of his meetings. Among these were 'My sins went rolling away', 'Travelling on the good old way' and 'That's what makes me glad'. He is also the author of the congregational song, 'I have found a great salvation'.

He was once a secretary to the Founder, with whom he twice travelled round the world, and also served as a secretary and travelling companion to Commissioner Thomas McKie. During the 1st World War the Brigadier brought cheer to thousands of British troops serving in France and Belgium, and was thanked by King George V at Buckingham Palace. At the outbreak of the 2nd World War, although seventy-five years of age, he offered his services again and was in charge of a Red Shield club at a British bomber station when he was promoted to Glory in 1944.

In 1878 John Lawley became the fortieth evangelist of The Christian Mission. He had no musical education or training, but sang as naturally 'as do the lark and the blackbird', to quote Richard Slater. His gifts as a successful prayer meeting leader reached the ears of Bramwell Booth, who passed on the information to his father. This led to the Founder's sending for Lawley, who was then stationed in Scotland, putting him up on the platform to 'take over' in one of his meetings and then asking him if he would be prepared to give himself up entirely to help the General in his public work.

Lawley's answer was immediate. 'By the grace of God', he said, 'I will live to be a fisher of men'. Thus began a partnership between William Booth and his ADC which lasted for twenty-two years, a God-blessed ministry that ended only with the Founder's promotion to Glory in 1912. Commissioner Lawley continued to serve General Bramwell Booth in the same loving way.

Lawley's talent as a 'sweet singer in Israel' greatly added to his meeting leadership. 'Sing it again, Lawley!', the Founder's frequent demand, has passed into Army phraseology. Many of his own songs were first used as solos in the General's meetings and have come into congregational use.

When the Commissioner first sang 'Hark, hear the Saviour knocking', with the chorus immediately taken up by the congregation, the old General quietly moved to the soloist's side and whispered, 'That will sing its way round the world'. Another song, 'My sins rose as high as a mountain', was introduced at a day's meetings held in the Queen's Hall, London.

An experience of which Commissioner Lawley loved to speak was his visit with the Founder to the Holy Land in 1905. A short time before, whilst standing by the conductor of a street car in Berlin, the idea of the song, ' 'Twas all for me', came to him. In 1912 Lawley remembered: 'This song came to mind more than any other when I was in the Holy Land. In Bethlehem I knelt on the spot where a star has been let into the ground to mark the manger's position and sang the first verse:

> The King of kings was in a stable born,
> 'Twas all for me . . .

'At Calvary, looking over the valley towards Jerusalem—as He did when He died—I sang the third verse:

> The Son of God was left alone to die,
> 'Twas all for me . . .'

Although Lawley is often given the credit for having written 'When Jesus was born in a manger', he did, in fact, write only the fourth and fifth verses. William Booth was shown the original song when he and his party were travelling in Queensland, Australia. He liked the first verse and chorus, but not the remainder of the song. Lawley was told to write new words. When the axle of one of the railway coaches became heated, causing a delay, Lawley stood on the platform and sang the additional verses while the General listened from the carriage window.

'There is a better land' was written in Norway whilst viewing the wonders of nature to be found in the 'land of the midnight sun'. 'O happy, happy day' was completed on a Petrograd to Berlin train just as it reached the Russian frontier. The Founder had been speaking at a drawing room meeting attended by the Czarina of Russia.

Lawley's last song, 'Though thunders roll and darkened be the sky', penned during his long, painful illness, was sung for the first time at his funeral service, conducted by General Bramwell Booth at Clapton Congress Hall on 14 September 1922. In his moving tribute, the General said, 'He sang his way through this life and he will sing his way through eternity. His was a ministry of song'. It was fitting that John Lawley's song book should have rested on the coffin on his last journey to Abney Park, together with his cap and Bible.

The natural successor to Commissioner Lawley was Colonel Joseph Pugmire. He became an officer from the small North of England corps of Penrith and served in the United States, Canada and at the International Training College. Like Lawley, Colonel Pugmire will be remembered mainly as the leader of prayer meetings in the great gatherings conducted by the Army's Generals in all parts of the world. His skilful intermingling of songs, solos and prayers made him a master in the art of soul-winning.

During his service in Canada, he became known as the Army's 'Minstrel to the prisoners' as he visited eighty penitentiaries across the vast Dominion. His favourite song, and theirs, was 'Sunshine on the hill'. Interviewed during a holiday in his homeland in 1911, he thought that this song had done more to lift the spirits of men in the cells and to give them new hope than any he had ever sung.

This song became a campaign theme when the Colonel became ADC to General Edward Higgins and accompanied him on his travels in the 1930s. There was a much-reported occasion in 1932 when 'Sunshine on the hill' was featured as a quartet in Canberra, Australia, the singers being General Higgins, Colonel Pugmire, the Governor-General and the Prime Minister.

If unpredictable in time and rhythm observance, Pugmire sang from his heart. Who old enough to remember his technique can forget his prayer meeting ministry? He would start to sing, often without waiting for support from the piano or organ, and then, when he felt so led, he would stop singing to reiterate the words and make an appeal to the unconverted. When he thought his sermonette should end he would continue to sing from the place where he had left the song—and was always on key.

On big occasions, like Royal Albert Hall days, he was at his best. It was not unusual for him to pause in the singing of a soulful refrain to announce, 'Another lift-load coming, General', as seekers streamed down the aisle from the back of the great auditorium toward the Mercy Seat. Active in this way in the early days of Army recordings, Colonel Pugmire's powerful, persuasive voice has been preserved in such favourites as 'I have pleasure in His service' and 'I heard a Voice so gently calling'.

The period between the two great wars brought to light a formidable array of gifted individual singers. The advent of the more sophisticated type of festival provided avenues for more advanced solos, but the high ideals of soulful interpretation were never neglected. Foremost in this category was Lieut.-Colonel Eva Fouracre who, after gaining a gold medal for singing in her teens and sacrificing prospects of a professional career, became an officer in 1922. The Colonel was the featured soloist in many national events in the 1930's, one of the highlights being the presentation, in manuscript, of 'Happy am I', the prize-winning vocal solo entered for the 1932 international composers' and songwriters' competition.

Two solos, 'My Desire' and 'O live Thy life in me', were recorded in the days when, with the arrival at a high note, the soloist was expected to turn away from the microphone so as not to break the sound barrier!

Other noted soprano soloists of that era were Mrs Lieut.-Colonel Thomas Ward and Mrs Brigadier Lilian Coulter, a converted opera singer. Both were featured at festivals at the Crystal Palace and other centres, as well as in meetings led by Army leaders. Mrs Ward recorded 'I know a fount' and 'Thou art enough for me', and Mrs Coulter's voice has been perpetuated on record in such Army gems as 'The penitent's plea'. 'The cross is not greater than His grace' and 'A perfect trust', among others.

The outstanding contralto soloist at this time was Doris Coles (Mrs Prout). Her rich singing was in great demand in these years and she was a member of General Evangeline Booth's vocal team which accompanied her on her first motorcade in Britain in 1935. Other vocalists used by the General on this campaign were Envoy Israel Cradle, from South Wales, Staff-Bandsman Alfred Andrews and

Songster Henry Kniveton. The three male singers were also featured
the following year when the General repeated her motorcade, this
time from Land's End to John o' Groats.

A noted bass soloist during these fruitful years was Songster Leader
Samuel Hooper, already referred to in a previous chapter. His
speciality solo, 'The Old Drummer', was featured up and down
Britain and was recorded, with Eric Ball, his friend of many years'
standing, at the piano.

Other territories were busy discovering their own vocal soloists.
Lieut.-Colonel Walter Mabee and Brigadier Ransom Gifford, of the
United States, visited London at different times, providing solos in
meetings conducted by General Evangeline. Brigadier Gifford
recorded 'I bring Thee all' and 'O save me, dear Lord'.

Then there was Adjutant Sven Simmonson, of Sweden, who sang in
the Bandmasters' Councils Festival in the Royal Albert Hall in 1937.
The bands were seated in the arena and a special podium was erected
near the International Staff Band so that the Adjutant could stand
close to the band as, under the sympathetic baton of Colonel George
Fuller, it accompanied him. 'Grace there is my every debt to pay',
with a delightfully arranged backing to the old melody, silenced the
audience and revealed evangelical singing at its dedicated best.

After the 2nd World War came Rita Green, Winnie Watson, June
Peach (Mrs Major Leslie Mingay) and Lawrence Mallyon in England;
Mrs Lieut.-Colonel Paul Anefelt and Gustav Kolm in Sweden, and a
host of others who achieved international recognition through visits to
other territories.

The good work continues.

CHAPTER TWENTY-TWO

LET THE MEN SING!

THE singing of men's voices, whether in unison or harmony, has always had a warm place in the hearts of Salvationists. Its development in organized form can be dated from around 1911.

At first quartet parties began to be formed. One of the earliest was at Carlisle Citadel. These vocal enthusiasts soon earned a name for themselves and in 1912 were invited to take part in the bandmasters' councils' festival at Clapton. That year they shared the male voice honours with Pentre Band, which travelled from the Rhondda Valley not only to play, but to blaze a trail of full-throated part-singing so typical of Welshmen. 'O how He loves', to the tune of 'All through the night', one verse in English and another in Welsh, so captivated the audience that some minutes elapsed before the next item could proceed.

Other quartet parties were quick to follow, particularly at Salisbury and Abertillery. In other places octet parties were formed and one or two more ambitious bands ventured to emulate Pentre's example in band singing.

One of the best-known octet parties of a bygone era was that at Clapton Congress Hall. The original group was formed away from the famous East London stronghold. A number of corps bandsmen found themselves in the same unit of His Majesty's Forces in the early days of the 1st World War and decided to get together to form a singing party. The leader was Adjutant (later Colonel) Ernest Wellman, later the corps bandmaster and Deputy Bandmaster of the International Staff Band.

The 'Army boys', as they were called, were in demand at secular and sacred concerts arranged for the troops. Overseas drafts meant splitting up the singers, but in 1919 five of them found themselves on the Congress Hall platform and were asked to sing. Their reception was so hearty that it was decided to keep the party going.

The original members of the octet as established in 'demob' days were Will Hopkins, Norman Cole, Will Holmes, Percy McLean, Gordon Wellman, Ernest Wellman, Alfred Ives and Oswald Lawley. They had their successors, but the singing went on well into the 1930s, with Colonel Wellman still in charge and his deputy bandmaster, Will Holmes, still adding the burlesque touches, with accompanying facial expressions. 'It's an old Army custom' and 'The

Army band' became side-splitting classics of good fun and relaxed happy fellowship.

Regent Hall Band took an interest in singing much earlier. In 1897 there was a vocal-instrument quartet functioning at festivals and on other occasions. The leader was Deputy Bandmaster Herbert Twitchin and the members were Louis Bocker, who sang 'Abide with me' in the forecourt of Buckingham Palace when the band played there at the request of Queen Alexandra following the death of King Edward VII in 1910; Fred Kinghorn, Arthur Light and 'Bert' Twitchin. A year later Ensign Arthur Goldsmith, possessed of an exceptionally deep voice, took over from Light.

Twitchin wrote many original songs for the quartet, including 'The great eternal remedy' and 'The march to heaven'. The first one was inspired by an advert he had seen whilst on honeymoon. It read: 'Get Jake's Compound. The great vegetable remedy. For all men's ills'.

Richard Slater rated 'H.W.T.' highly as a creator of melody and persuaded him to visit seaside concert parties while on holiday, to catch the spirit of their rollicking songs and to write similar material for Army purposes.

This the young composer did to good effect and the few published works from his pen became among the most widely used of all Army vocal music. It is regretted that his busy life did not permit Bandmaster Twitchin to bequeath more song melodies to succeeding generations of Salvationists.

After the 2nd World War, when Band Sergeant Will Holmes transferred from Clapton Congress Hall to Regent Hall, an excellent vocal octet was formed, on the lines of the famous Congress Hall singers, and existed for quite a while.

The Abertillery quartet was first formed in 1917 and, after participating in a London national festival in the early 1920s, was selected to feature a song on General Bramwell Booth's last broadcast service from London 2LO station in 1928. When Abertillery Band campaigned at Southampton for Easter week-end, 1956, that broadcasting quartet again functioned on the programmes. They were the brothers Raymond and Vincent Veal, James Mason and Cyril Harding. All were Tonic sol-fa experts, the Veals featuring well-known Army marches transposed into the system and performed at lightning speed.

Not surprisingly, Welsh Salvationists led the way in full band singing. In the first bandmasters' councils festival after the 1st World War, Blaina Band took part and, during meetings conducted by General Bramwell the following day, introduced an Army congregation to 'Guide me, O Thou great Jehovah', sung to the stirring 'Cwm Rhondda'. It was a sensation.

A year later Pentre Band, led by Bandmaster William Walker, composer of the popular male voice song, 'Jerusalem', played two pieces and sang 'Friend of sinners' and 'Comrades in arms'. At councils the next day one of the highlights was the singing by all the Welsh delegates of 'Who is on the Lord's side?' to 'Rachie'.

'Before the chorus had been sung the third time', reported *The Bandsman and Songster,* 'the seed was well planted and the roof of the lecture hall vibrated with the well-known words to a new and striking tune. At breakfast the next morning the visitors sang it again, and by now the tune will have reached the four corners of the land where it will remain a valuable instrument in proclaiming the glory of God.' Prophetic words indeed!

No group of men has given a greater lead to male chorus singing than the International Staff Band. This was first featured during the bandmastership of Eric Ball, during the middle years of the 2nd World War, and continued when, under the leadership of Lieut.-Colonel William Stewart, the Deputy Bandmaster (Colonel Bernard Adams) became responsible for the singing.

A high standard of singing by the band has been maintained during the thirty intervening years, first under the leadership of Colonel Adams for twenty-eight years and now directed by the present Bandmaster (Major Ray Bowes).

Colonel Adams has served as Songster Leader at Upper Norwood for many years, and when General Clarence Wiseman admitted him to the Order of the Founder upon his retirement from the Staff Band in 1975, the citation stated that in addition to his ISB bandmastership he had 'served wholeheartedly as a local officer'.

The band's long line of soloists would make an impressive male voice party were they all alive today. Names that come to mind include Harry Green, Samuel Hurren, Charles Coller, Arthur Goldsmith, Edgar Dibden and Joseph Reardon. Before his conversion, Lieut.-Colonel Reardon regularly sang at secular concerts and it was while he was singing a song that contained a skit on The Salvation Army that conviction struck him.

Shortly afterwards he attended an Army meeting and knelt at the Mercy Seat in penitence. Not only was he an effective soloist with the ISB, but at times he also featured in duets with his brother Jim, who was a member of the Staff Band at the same time. History repeated itself when Joseph's sons, Maurice and Terence, began to sing vocal duets. The brothers took part in this way in meetings at their corps, Penge, and in national events at Clapton Congress Hall.

After the 1st World War the ranks of Staff Band vocalists were increased with such personalities as Herbert Barker, Alfred Andrews, David Wolfe, George Prowse and Albert Barnett. Later still came Ronald Symonds, Campbell Robinson, William Binns, Leslie Condon and Elgar Gambling.

Like its counterpart in London, the New York Staff Band Male Chorus has an impressive record of service. As the USA National Staff Band, this group took part in the 1914 International Congress and, among other activities, sang at the graves of William Booth and the Army Mother in Abney Park Cemetery.

Colonel William Darby, who was Bandmaster at Cannock (England) until he left for America in 1907, was the chorus leader from 1914 to 1930, serving as Staff Bandmaster for an even longer period. The Colonel consistently set the standard of first-class vocal music in the Eastern Territory and his tradition has been carried on faithfully by a number of effective male chorus leaders, some of whom trained under his sensitive direction. Colonel Darby also led the Staff Songsters in New York for many years.

The present Commissioner Richard Holz, a former Bandmaster of the New York Staff Band, conducted the Male Chorus for nine years before handing over to the then Captain Vernon Post, who was the leader when the band visited Britain in 1960 and 1968. Commissioner Holz has always taken vocal interests extremely seriously and set a standard of excellence that will long be remembered.

The New York Staff Band Male Chorus has been fortunate in its vocal soloists. The rich, deep tones of Envoy Frank Fowler were heard in the band's festivals and in countless devotional meetings for fifty-eight years—1899 to 1957—and he was proud of a record of service which included singing in campaigns conducted in New York by six of the Army's Generals.

Frank Fowler was in London with the band for both the 1904 and 1914 Congresses, and one of his great ambitions came true in 1957 when the International Staff Band visited the USA for the first time and members of the two bands were able to share fellowship.

Another outstanding vocalist of the band was Lieut.-Colonel Olof Lundgren, now retired from banding. He served for more than twenty years as the tenor soloist and became renowned for his masterly interpretation of 'Banners and Bonnets' and Erik Leidzén's 'A man may be down but he is never out'.

The name of Major Albert Avery is still remembered for his telling solo, with band vocal accompaniment, featured during the New York Staff Band's participation in the 1960 bandmasters' councils festival. This was 'Rock of Ages', an arrangement by a former Bandmaster,

Lieut.-Colonel William Bearchell. The Major is still a member of the band.

Major Peter Hofman has made a substantial contribution to the history of the male chorus. Apart from Staff Band vocal service, he is well known outside the Army for his tenor feature, with voice and ensemble support from the Staff Band, of the record, 'There's still time, brother', from the film, 'On the beach'.

United male chorus singing has not been lacking on either side of the Atlantic, nor in other parts of the world. In England this type of vocal variety has been included in national songster festivals and councils' festivals at the Royal Albert Hall and other centres. The singing of 'What shall the answer be?' at the 1967 Festival of Sounding Praise and 'When Jesus looked o'er Galilee', to the tune of 'Fewster', sung at a festival during the British Congress meetings at Wembley Pool in 1972, are cases in point.

Forty years ago male singing on such a scale was quite unknown. In London it was General Evangeline Booth who started the fashion. Newly arrived at the international centre, she was announced to give her famous lecture, 'The Romance of The Salvation Army', in the Royal Albert Hall. She asked for a male chorus to give vocal support at intervals in the script. The General had received such help from the New York Staff Band on previous occasions. Colonel Railton Howard was given the task of recruiting vocalists from officers and employees serving at the Associated Headquarters in London. The days when bandsmen from a wide area were able to take hours off work had not yet arrived!

Three headquarters bands then in operation—the ISB and those of the Men's Social Headquarters and Salvationist Publishing & Supplies, Ltd.—formed the nucleus of the group and other available personnel were added to make up the required numbers.

This meant a full day's absence from duty. In the morning the songs, produced in manuscript form and distributed upon arrival, were learned and the seating formation was finalized. Balance proved a problem at first, but the long experience of Colonel Ernest Wellman came to the rescue when he suggested that perhaps a better effect could be produced if each row contained a complete four-part chorus of its own, instead of the usual method of having each part grouped in a mass.

Colonel Howard accepted the advice, and there was no further trouble. Many present that morning remembered this experiment when in later years they came to conduct mass male voice singing!

After lunch the General arrived for a rehearsal and patiently tested the acoustics and repeated the parts of the lecture affecting the singing background over and over again until she was satisfied. 'It's important', she kept saying.

In the evening, while the packed audience sat rigidly under the spell of her oratory, the General stood for more than an hour, her personal flag clasped in her hand, every inflection of the voice and gesture of the hand having meaning. With only the occasional dramatic well-timed pause to interrupt the amazing flow of language, and without a note to prompt her should she need it, she unfolded the glorious Salvation Army story, touching upon every facet of its complex construction with a knowledge and skill that few in the Movement can have surpassed.

And the male chorus sat intent, waiting for the familiar up-beat of Colonel Howard to stir them into action with 'O boundless salvation', 'Bowed beneath a garden shade', 'Sun of my soul' or 'Rescue the perishing'.

Evangeline Booth was certainly her father's daughter. His gift for dramatic presentation had descended upon her, and she too learned to use it to the glory of God and the betterment of The Salvation Army. Her lovely smile, flourish of the hand, and affectionate incline of the head toward the 'gentlemen of the chorus' as she left the platform amidst the lingering cheers was all the reward they wanted for a long, tiring, often frustrating day.

CHAPTER TWENTY-THREE

MELODIES OF YOUTH

THE variety of names given to Salvation Army vocal groups in earlier days makes it impossible for any historian to alight upon a likely date which marked the beginning of young people's singing companies. The first reference to what could have been such a group appears in *The Bandsman and Songster,* November 1910.

Brigadier Richard Slater reported that he had been to Chalk Farm for a festival in which all four music sections of the corps took part. The band (Bandmaster A. W. Punchard) was already internationally known for its overseas trips; the six-year-old songster brigade was doing well under its founder-leader, Edward Souter; the junior brass band, for the first time, was permitted to share a programme with the senior section; and the 'junior singing brigade' participated with a three-part song, 'Shout, shout aloud'.

There were some junior vocalists active at St Albans in 1914, but this was an all-male affair. During the preceding summer this band of lads had spent their Saturday afternoons exploring the neighbouring countryside, under the designation of the junior rambling brigade, and in the winter months, to maintain the interest, they formed themselves into a male voice singing brigade.

Singing companies, as they are known today, officially came into being in the early 1920s when regulation uniform was introduced. This consisted of navy dress, or white blouse, with blue velour hats bearing a distinctive badge on the front. A yellow, red and blue sash worn across the dress or blouse completed the uniform. This has been modified considerably with the passing of the years and the headgear particularly has undergone many changes in the process of frequent up-dating attempts.

The most ambitious effort to involve large numbers of singing company members in a national event up to that time came to fruition at the Alexandra Palace National Youth Day in June 1935. Singing companies from the five London divisions were formed into separate groups, each participating as a single unit. The leaders chosen for this experiment were Adjutant Idwal Evans (South-West); Captain Wesley Evans (West); Adjutant George Higgins (North); Songster Leader Joseph Long (East London). Adjutant Evans was the Commanding Officer at Brixton, his brother at Maidenhead, and Adjutant Higgins at Hendon.

The honour of being the first singing company in Britain to broadcast goes to that of Bridgeton. During the first visit to London of this Scottish group, in 1935, the leader and members were introduced in the popular national wavelength feature, 'In town tonight'. The following year the singing company visited Northern Ireland and sang from the Belfast studio. In two years this fine group of youthful singers travelled some 3,000 miles. The leader was Young People's Sergeant-Major John Gibbs.

Another busy singing company at that time was Edmonton (Canada), its leader being Young People's Sergeant-Major William Eadie. In 1937 the singers undertook a ten-day tour through Southern Alberta, covering a distance of nearly 1,000 miles, conducting fourteen open-air meetings and twenty-three indoor meetings and festivals, and broadcasting from Calgary and Lethbridge.

A second outstanding Canadian singing company hit the headlines after the 2nd World War. This was the group from Hamilton, Ontario, which had come into being during the war years and had been well trained by their efficient, qualified leader, Mrs Mabel McFarlane. The singing company leader hails from Penge and is the daughter of Adjutant Howse, who was a pioneer in Army film-making in London, in 1903.

Although the first music camp in Army history came into being at Long Branch, New Jersey, USA, in 1921, it was not until 1936 that vocal studies were introduced into the programme. The year before, Commissioner John J. Allan, the Long Branch pioneer, inaugurated the famous Star Lake camp. The Territorial Music Director, Captain (later Commissioner) Richard Holz, was responsible for the innovation and greatly encouraged vocal development, as well as instrumental, until he relinquished musical work in New York to take up another appointment in 1963.

Music camps in Canada followed in 1940, and Jackson's Point, Ontario, has remained the main centre of the territory's instrumental and vocal activity among budding musicians.

The first singing company camp in Britain came in 1948. A year before, Hadleigh had been the site of the first band camp and the vocal enthusiasts among prominent songster leaders did not want to be left behind in this commendable forward move. When the British Commissioner (Commissioner William Dalziel) received a letter from Songster Leader Muriel Wilson, of Nelson, he saw the point of her request that urgent effort should be made to rectify the omission of plans for youthful vocalists. This resulted in the first camp in August 1948, at Sunbury Court.

In this idyllic setting 100 girls from singing companies in the

British Territory gathered for a week to enjoy happy fellowship, learn the art of singing and put that learning into practice. The camp director was Brigadier (later Commissioner) Kaare Westergaard, then National Young People's Secretary, and the music director was Brigadier (later Colonel) Mrs Ivy Mawby, already well known as a songwriter. The team of pioneer instructors included Lieut.-Colonel Wesley Evans and the young woman who plucked up courage to write to the Commissioner, Songster Leader Wilson (now Mrs William Yendell), of Hendon.

The final week-end was spent at Chalk Farm, the entire company first making a private recording at a West End studio in the morning and then paying a visit to the London Zoo.

The success was repeated the next year and became a fixture on the calendar of young vocalists from all parts of the country and overseas. In 1978 British vocal music camps celebrated their thirtieth anniversary.

For many years the genial, lovable 'Uncle Sam' Hooper was an able instructor and Muriel Yendell served as Music Director for a long time, until her heavy responsibilities as a headmistress made it necessary for her to withdraw from the work she had pioneered and loved to carry through for so many years. Her successor was Bandmaster Donald Osgood, of Southall, a sensitive and demanding musician who maintained the high standards established by his predecessors. Songster Leader Fred Crowhurst, of Birmingham Citadel, has given excellent support in recent years.

The singing company camps became summer schools of music in 1958 and the raising of the age limits meant that young songsters were eligible. In that year a twenty-one-year-old mother was among the students, probably unwittingly making history.

In 1977 the National Schools of Music in Britain went co-educational, the scene of this amalgamation being Cobham Hall, Kent. A joint festival was given at Fairfield Halls, Croydon, at the end of the week and the exceedingly high standard of both instrumentalists and vocalists told its own story. General Arnold Brown was the chairman, this being his first public engagement since his welcome as General in the Westminster Central Hall four days before. Boys and girls sang in this meeting.

Britain's first divisional singing camp was held in 1953 at Grendon Hall, Northamptonshire, for vocalists of the East Midlands Division. These have continued ever since, under the musical direction of such personalities as Songster Leaders Muriel Yendell, Freda Lambert and Maisie Wiggins. The next year music camps spread to Scotland where

Lieut.-Colonel Rance, then National Secretary for Bands and Songster Brigades, directed the musical operations.

Following the change in designation to music schools, regional events were announced, but a system designed to enable the top girls from these schools to graduate to the national schools never materialized.

In 1964 Wales had its first music school—and went co-educational from the start. The Music Director was Major Dean Goffin, and the singing leaders were Songster Leader Rosetta Williams, of Pentre, and Young People's Singing Company Leader Mrs Ivor Bosanko, of Cardiff Canton. Jeanette Bosanko is now serving with her husband in New York City, where she is maintaining her reputation as a vocal soloist. Subsequent directors of the Welsh school include Major Norman Bearcroft and Major Leslie Condon.

Two English singing companies have conducted campaigns on the Continent of Europe: Clapton Congress Hall in Switzerland in 1958, with Mrs General Frederick Coutts (then Lieut.-Colonel Olive Gattrall) as International Headquarters representative, and North Shields in Norway ten years later.

A group called the London Girl Songsters was formed to take part in the bandmasters' councils' festival of 1955. It was composed of songsters under twenty-one years of age drawn from the London divisions, with Songster Leader Mrs Yendell as conductor. It was an instant success and before the end of the year had a number of recordings to its credit. The group functioned for some two years, during which more recordings were made, and in 1960 some of the members became the founder singers of the National Songsters.

Several recordings have also been made of the Sunbury Junior Singers, led by Major Joy Webb. 'Hymns for little children' was the first and all have been popular. The vocalists were students of the Junior National Schools of Music, which Major Webb has directed for some years.

In 1977 a new departure at this annual event allowed the presentation of the Major's mini-musical, *Little Teacher,* based upon the life of Adjutant Catherine Hine, of London's Chinatown. The delightful songs provided ample material for vocal instruction during the week, and this 'course with a difference' succeeded in holding the attention of the young people. Public performances were presented at Regent Hall and Wood Green.

A popular company of youthful singers who started making vocal music together in 1951 was the Students' Fellowship Choral Group. Its leader was Douglas Collin, who had recently graduated from Cambridge University and taken a teaching post in London. They met at the Army's West Central Hotel, Southampton Row, talked about the idea and decided that they would gather prior to meetings of the fellowship, just to sing for their own interest and blessing. The singers began with 'How sweet the name of Jesus sounds', to the tune of 'Lloyd', and immediately discovered the sheer delight to be derived from unaccompanied four-part small-group singing.

The first engagement was at the Students' Fellowship annual week-end at Regent Hall, and they were soon receiving invitations to special. Participation in festivals at the Royal Albert Hall, the Colston Hall, Bristol, and Westminster Central Hall followed, and because of their size—they never numbered more than twenty-one—they were able to visit small corps.

Their first broadcast was as a background to the BBC morning feature, 'Lift up your hearts', conducted for a week in 1953 by Lieut.-Colonel Harry Dean. Later they provided a programme of songs for 'Epilogue' and also broadcast on the BBC Overseas Service.

This small but efficient group lasted for some eight years, the final week-end being spent at Edinburgh Gorgie Corps. It disbanded when Songster Leader and Mrs Collin left for Christian service in Northern Rhodesia (now Zambia). Here the infectious enthusiast continued his vocal interests by forming a choir at the David Livingstone Teacher Training College.

CHAPTER TWENTY-FOUR

RHYTHM FINDS ITS GROOVE

FIRST pronouncements are important. When interviewed on the radio following his election as General, Albert Orsborn likened post-war Salvationists to efficient bulldozers, then to be seen on the streets of London clearing the rubble and helping to rebuild the city. The slogan he gave was, 'Put the Army on wheels, and if necessary on wings'.

Seventeen years later General Frederick Coutts, in similar circumstances, expressed the hope that The Salvation Army might show a more modern approach to the old task of bringing the message of the Christian faith to the 'man in the street'. Pressed further by the interviewer, the newly-elected General said that, alongside the ministry of the brass band, it should be possible to take the message of salvation to coffee bars with electric guitars if this proved to be an effective method.

Next morning the daily newspapers 'went to town'. Cartoonists had a field day. One of them depicted a group holding an open-air meeting while disillusioned bandsmen retreated with battered brass instruments underneath their arms, the guitars of the usurpers clumsily plugged into the street lighting system by means of exaggerated lengths of electric lead.

The whole idea attracted considerable publicity and the Press wanted to see photographs of Salvationists using the new 'sound'. The officer at International Headquarters responsible for such liaison matters was nonplussed. There were no groups, but the request provided too good a chance to miss. What could he do?

The International Training College at Denmark Hill supplied an answer. On the staff was a capable young officer, Captain Joy Webb. Possessed of a good singing voice and gifted with an aptitude for anything musical, the Captain was asked to find some girls who had brought guitars with them into training. This was done, and the unsuspecting victims, with Captain Webb, were taken on a round tour of Westminster to find a suitable background.

Joy Webb remembers: '*Time* magazine put us outside No. 10 Downing Street and right on to their front cover. We were taken along to the Houses of Parliament and photographed at all angles with Big Ben in the background. There was no end to it.'

This was not the first attempt of modern Salvationists to get 'with it'. In 1957 a party of cadets from the training college conducted an

autumn campaign in Leicester. An enterprising leader 'cashed in' on
'skiffle', forming a group with harmonicas, combs, guitars, tambourines, and even a washboard. This was in keeping with a recent
craze popularized by pop star Lonnie Donegan.

An open-air meeting happened to be held outside the offices of
the *Leicester Evening Mail*. A reporter on the staff of that paper saw
them and sensed a story. As a result the personal initiative of the
cadets received considerable publicity in the national press the next
morning. Later that month a similar group, with Captain Webb on
her accordion, appeared on BBC television.

In March 1962, following a *War Cry* article by General Wilfred
Kitching, in which he stated that Salvationists must do more about
reaching the masses, a septet of Army musicians presented a
programme at Thornton Heath. This was geared to members of youth
clubs and other young people invited from local coffee bars.

'Salvation Swing' was back again, accompanied by the anticipated
bout of controversy. Letters published in *The Musician* revealed that
opinions were sharply divided and that tact and tolerance would be
required on the part of leaders and enthusiastic executants.

Support immediately came from Australia and South Africa, in
which countries guitars were being used effectively in the cause of
youth evangelism. A group of 'youth strings' formed in Sweden was
soon featured on television. In New York a similar combination was
reported as singing in a Broadway night club.

This was the situation at the time of General Coutts's election and
pronouncement. An invitation to appear on the BBC feature,
'Tonight', was accepted with reasonable nervousness. It was difficult
for Cliff Michelmore to introduce the cadets because they had no
name. The idea had never occurred to them or anyone else.

As they sang their songs that evening a director of the EMI
company was viewing and listening in his home. He liked what he saw
and heard, and set the ball rolling. A week or two later, Joy Webb and
the cadets were asked to go to the studios to make a test recording. The
group's first record, a forty-five single disc, was released on 14
February 1964. The songs were 'We're going to set the world a-
singing' and 'It's an open secret', both written and composed by Joy
Webb.

The second song came to birth in a meeting at the college when
the wife of the Training Principal, now Mrs General Clarence
Wiseman, shared with the staff some words from a book of
paraphrased New Testament readings. Paul had written, 'Our love for
Christ is an open secret'. That first disc has another claim to Army
music history. On it appeared the name 'Joystrings' for the first time.

It was Mr Robert Dockerill, of EMI and a good Army friend for many years, who said the group must have a name for recording purposes. As Colonel Bernard Adams, Manager of the Musical Publications and Instruments Department at Salvationist Publishing and Supplies Ltd, Colonel Charles Skinner, Head of the International Music Editorial Department, and Robert Dockerill discussed the matter over a cup of tea the inspired title was born.

Not that the name could be used extensively. It was officially taboo for a long time. Army periodicals were instructed to refer merely to 'The International Training College Rhythm Group'. In bolder moments editors were courageous enough to add 'for recording purposes known as the Joystrings'.

The record made an immediate impact. 'Captain Joy' became a national figure overnight. Her first 'solo' appearance on radio was on Jimmy Young's 'Saturday Special'. The record was played and the Captain was interviewed. Next came a request to record for another radio programme. It was 24 February 1964. The scene was the EMI studios in London's West End. There was an audience. The crowd of teenagers hoping for admission, although they had been unsuccessful in securing tickets, could not believe their eyes as they saw a group of eight young people in Salvation Army uniform approaching. 'Are you playing here tonight?', they asked incredulously as the Salvationists made their way through the throng toward the entrance.

Inside the low-roofed theatre-studio some 100 young pop enthusiasts prepared to enjoy and participate in the sixty-minute 'Friday Spectacular' show to be broadcast from Radio Luxembourg that week. Toward the end of the show the Joystrings were generously introduced by the compère, Shaw Taylor, and were listened to with reservation which soon turned to unanimous approval as 'It's an open secret' proceeded. The storm of applause which greeted the group at the record's conclusion was overwhelming, prompting a 'Wow! Wow!' from the compère.

The Joystrings could hold their heads high. That day their first disc had reached a place on the national charts. They had invaded the pop empire and conquered. A double success.

When Joy Webb appeared on the Jimmy Young show the group was given a 'plug' by the announcement that their first public performance was to take place at Camberwell. This no doubt helped to pack the hall with an audience sixty per cent of which were estimated to be teenagers. The 'performance' ended with a Bible reading, words of appeal and several young people kneeling at the Penitent-form. This memorable meeting set the pattern for all meetings and campaigns conducted by the Joystrings.

The invitation to play in the cabaret at the 'Blue Angel' Club made headlines in the Press all over the world. The group was permitted to accept and to play for three nights. The first appearance is vividly described by Joy:

'At midnight we made our way to the club, and about 3 am were standing in the wings waiting to go on. It was a sight to remember. One fellow, commenting on the crush, said, "I've been to some opening nights, but I've never seen so many pressmen in the 'Blue Angel' Club—ever before, for anything!"

'The club was packed far beyond capacity. Pressmen hung from parts of the structure of the room. Television and film lights beat down mercilessly in an atmosphere already overcharged with heat . . . Marlene Dietrich gazed out of her picture with (was it my imagination?) mild amazement.'

Others shared the German film star's amazement. Among these were those, with tongues loosened by liquor, who stayed behind to talk with the Salvationists, sharing confidences, seeking spiritual advice, and asking help in unravelling domestic problems.

There was the blonde girl who was having trouble with her stiletto heels catching in the lace hem of her evening gown. She had imbibed too much drink, but was not too drunk to say, 'I never go to church, but I want to tell you that you dig the craziest and most wonderful gospel I've ever heard'.

Then there was the man who passed his menu nervously to the group to be autographed. He seemed in no hurry to leave. After chatting about the music for a time he suddenly blurted out, 'Of course, I used to be a Salvationist and you've made me remember the old days—and a lot more!'

It was not envisaged that the life of the Joystrings would last five years. Their days were, in fact, officially numbered at the time of the Army's Centenary Celebrations in the summer of 1965. Commissioner William Cooper, then the British Commissioner, had other ideas. A 'reprieve' was granted. Following the commissioning of two members, Peter Dalziel and Bill Davidson, as officers, the group was transformed to serve under the Commissioner's jurisdiction at National Headquarters. Other valued members were Lieutenant Sylvia Gair and Mrs Lieutenant Pauline Banks. In the three ensuing years the Joystrings reached their finest hour.

At the time of their transfer to National Headquarters administration, under the direction of the National Secretary for Bands and Songster Brigades, opposition to the Joystrings was at its strongest. Some Salvationists and other Christian friends were not wholly convinced of the rightness of the group's activity. One minister

Made and printed in Great Britain by
The Campfield Press, St Albans, Herts